diabetic slow cooker

151 cozy, comforting recipes

Houghton Mifflin Harcourt
Boston   New York

Copyright © 2012 by Meredith Corporation, Des Moines, IA. All rights reserved

Published by Houghton Mifflin Harcourt Publishing Company

Published simultaneously in Canada

For information about permission to reproduce selections from this book, write to trade.permissions@hmhco.com or to Permissions, Houghton Mifflin Harcourt Publishing Company, 3 Park Avenue, 19th Floor, New York, New York 10016.

www.hmhco.com

Library of Congress Cataloging-in-Publication Data is available upon request.

ISBN 978-1-118-34433-0 (pbk), ISBN 978-1-118-44174-9 (ebk), ISBN 978-1-118-44176-3 (ebk), ISBN 978-1-118-44178-7 (ebk)

Printed in China
SCP 10 9 8 7
4500657063

Meredith Corporation

Food & Nutrition Editor: Jessie Shafer

Contributing Project Manager: Shelli McConnell, Purple Pear Publishing, Inc.

Art Director: Michelle Bilyeu

Publisher: Natalie Chapman

Associate Publisher: Jessica Goodman

Executive Editor: Anne Ficklen

Editor: Adam Kowit

Senior Editorial Assistant: Heather Dabah

Production Director: Diana Cisek

Senior Production Editor: Amy Zarkos

Design and Layout: Tai Blanche and Indianapolis Composition Services

Manufacturing Manager: Tom Hyland

Our seal assures you that every recipe in *Diabetic Living® Diabetic Slow Cooker* has been tested in the Better Homes and Gardens® Test Kitchen. This means that each recipe is practical and reliable and meets our high standards of taste appeal. We guarantee your satisfaction with this book for as long as you own it.

Home Stretch

Getting dinner on the table is often the last hurdle in a day of jumping from task to task. That's why I'm especially thankful for this collection of healthful and hearty recipes that makes my mealtimes a little calmer and evenings a little easier. The slow cookers in the Better Homes and Gardens® Test Kitchen have been working overtime to dish out meaty stews and roasts, saucy sandwiches and pasta dishes, and potluck-ready appetizers. The best part: All of these recipes have been carb-counted and boosted with nutritious ingredients—so they're diabetes-friendly for you and tasty for everyone at the table!

I've been sneaking more than a few of these treasured recipes home to test on my pickiest taster: my husband. I can tell from his oohs and ahhs (and his scraped-clean plates) that this is a winning group of simmered dishes. Some standouts include a soothing bowl of Pork Zuppa (page 181), a tantalizing plate of Slow-"Roasted" Tomatoes (page 220), and one sweetly simple Chocolate Fondue (page 33). Whether you use your slow cooker for entertaining or easy dinners, potlucks or pots of leftovers, I know these recipes will bring comfort to your cravings and simplicity to your days. Enjoy!

Whether you're feeding a crowd or only two, we have recipes just your size! A favorite in my home? The Dijon Beef Stew on page 170.

Jessie

Jessie Shafer

Food & Nutrition Editor, *Diabetic Living*

table of contents

Slow Cooker Savvy

Find out how to get the most out of this simple-to-use, time-saving meal maker.

1 Meat Matters

- Never toss frozen raw meat directly into your slow cooker—the meat will thaw too slowly to remain safe to eat.

- Use the cut of meat called for in the recipe. Slow cookers are ideal for less-tender cuts; substituting a cut that is more tender (and more expensive) won't make the dish better.

- Trim excess fat from meat and poultry before cooking.

- Brown the meat as directed in recipes. Doing so adds flavor and color to the dish and makes draining off excess fat easy.

- Skim fat from the cooking liquid or sauce before serving it.

2 The Veggie Story

- Because vegetables cook more slowly than meats, cut the vegetables into uniform pieces and place them closest to the heat source.

- Add dense veggies, such as carrots, potatoes, and parsnips, at the beginning of the recipe. Add tender veggies, such as green beans, spinach, and zucchini, at the end of cooking. Cook according to recipe directions or on the high-heat setting for 30 minutes or until they are tender.

3 Fill 'Er Up (But Not Too Full)

- To cook safely, your cooker needs to be filled at least half full but no more than two-thirds full. If you omit an ingredient such as parsnips in a recipe, replace it with an equal amount of a similar ingredient such as carrots.

- If using a cooker larger than the recipe calls for, increase everything—from the meat and vegetables to the liquid and seasonings—proportionately, making sure the cooker is half to just two-thirds full. Cook for the time specified in the recipe.

4 Don't Peek!

- Put a lid on it—and keep it there. Every time you open the lid, you release valuable heat and moisture and add 30 minutes to the cooking time. (That's why glass lids are handy.)

- Keep in mind that hot steam will gather on the inside of the lid. To avoid burns, lift the lid gently and straight up without tilting until it's clear of the cooker.

5 Put It to the Test

Slow cookers can fail to heat properly as they age. To make sure your slow cooker is safe to use, fill it half to two-thirds with water. Heat the water, covered, on the low-heat setting for 8 hours. Check the water temperature with an accurate food thermometer. If the thermometer doesn't register around 185°F, then it's time to buy another cooker.

6 A Clean Machine

- Let the cooker cool to room temperature before washing to prevent it from cracking. If the liner is removable, wash it in the dishwasher. If not, clean the cooker with a soft cloth and soapy water. Never use abrasive cleaners or pads.

- For quick cleanup, look for nylon slow cooker liners. These fit most oval and round slow cookers with capacities of 3 to 6.5 quarts.

7 The Inside Secret

Slow cookers have electric coils that slowly cook foods at around 200°F on the low-heat setting and about 300°F on the high-heat setting. Cookers with heating elements embedded in the side cook food more evenly than those with the heating element below the food container. The recipes in this book were tested in slow cookers with heating elements in the side.

8 Cook Once/Eat Twice

Most slow-cooked recipes yield much-appreciated leftovers. Immediately after your meal, transfer the extra food to freezer containers and freeze up to 6 months. Thaw in the refrigerator or microwave.

Lighten Up the Slow Cooker

Giving your favorite slow cooker recipes a healthful makeover is easy. Here's how to trim those tried-and-true dishes and still enjoy the delicious flavors you crave.

1 Cut Sodium Down to Size

Reach for the right product at the store to cut the sodium significantly in recipes. For example, these canned products reduce the sodium by these amounts:

- **Save 200 mg** when you use reduced-sodium tomatoes instead of regular tomatoes (per ½ cup).

- **Save 290 mg** when you use reduced-sodium broth instead of regular chicken broth (per 1 cup).

- **Save 315 mg** when you use no-salt-added red kidney beans instead of regular kidney beans (per ½ cup).

2 Beef Up the Meat . . . with Vegetables

To add nutrients while cutting fat, go up on the veggies and down on the amount of meat you use in a recipe. For example:

- **Ground meat dishes:** When making sloppy joes, decrease the meat by one-fourth and make up the difference with nonstarchy veggies such as tomatoes, onions, sweet peppers, and mushrooms. Per ½ cup, you'll save 221 calories and 7 grams fat per serving.

- **Beef roasts:** Use a smaller cut than called for and increase the veggies to fill the cooker between half and one-third full. Use low-carb choices such as mushrooms, carrots, turnips, celery, onions, and green beans.

3 Let's Talk Turkey

Slim down chili and sloppy joes with turkey breast. Ground turkey breast handily beats 90 percent lean ground beef by 60 calories and 8 grams of fat per 3 ounces of raw meat. There's just one catch: Be sure to reach for ground turkey *breast;* ground turkey that includes skin and dark meat can have as much fat and calories as ground beef.

4 Nix the Seasoning Mixes (and Make Your Own!)

If a recipe calls for a seasoning mix or a packaged dry rub, dip mix, or salad dressing mix, beware: These can be sodium bombs. Make your own dry mix with herbs and spices you like—and use a very light hand with the salt. You'll save anywhere from 250 to 500 mg of sodium per serving when using homemade versus purchased dry mixes.

5 Count Down—with Lower-Fat Products

These ingredient substitutions reduce fat and calories.

When you use	You'll save
Light coconut milk instead of regular	206 calories and 23 g fat per ½ cup
Reduced-fat, reduced-sodium condensed cream of mushroom soup instead of regular	30 calories, 4.5 g fat, and 410 g sodium per ½ cup
Light sour cream instead of regular	53 calories and 9 g fat per ½ cup
Reduced-fat cream cheese (Neufchâtel) instead of regular	51 calories and 6 g fat per ½ cup

6 Factor in Some Fiber

Boosting the fiber of any recipe is as easy as stirring a can of rinsed and drained no-salt-added beans, such as black, white, or red beans, into a recipe. You'll add about 5 grams of fiber per serving, which is about one-fifth of your daily needs. Just be sure you don't fill your cooker more than two-thirds full.

party bites

Looking for a great excuse for a party? With these recipes, spicy wings, gooey dips, tantalizing meatballs, and other favorite party foods can definitely fit in with your aim to eat well. That's something to celebrate!

Thai Chicken Wings with Peanut Sauce

3g CARB PER SERVING

PREP: 25 minutes **SLOW COOK:** 5 to 6 hours (low) or 2½ to 3 hours (high)
MAKES: 12 servings (2 drummettes and 2 teaspoons sauce each)

24 **chicken wing drummettes (about 2¼ pounds)**
¼ **cup water**
 1 **tablespoon lime juice**
¼ **teaspoon ground ginger**
 1 **recipe Peanut Sauce**

1. Place chicken in a 3½- or 4-quart slow cooker. Add the water, lime juice, and ginger to cooker.
2. Cover and cook on low-heat setting for 5 to 6 hours or on high-heat setting for 2½ to 3 hours.
3. Prepare Peanut Sauce. Drain chicken, discarding cooking liquid. Toss chicken with half of the Peanut Sauce. If desired, return chicken to slow cooker. Serve immediately or keep warm, covered, on warm-heat or low-heat setting for up to 1 hour. Serve with remaining sauce (whisk sauce if it looks separated).

Peanut Sauce: In a small saucepan whisk together ½ cup creamy peanut butter; ½ cup water; 2 tablespoons reduced-sodium soy sauce; 2 cloves garlic, minced; ½ teaspoon ground ginger; and ¼ teaspoon crushed red pepper. Heat over medium-low heat until mixture is smooth, whisking constantly.

PER SERVING: 101 cal., 6 g total fat (1 g sat. fat), 15 mg chol., 159 mg sodium, 3 g carb. (1 g fiber, 1 g sugars), 9 g pro. Exchanges: 1.5 lean meat, 1 fat.

Time-Saving Trick: Next time you're squeezing lemon or lime juice, squeeze some extra. Freeze the juice in ice cube trays until solid, then transfer the cubes to freezer bags. Thaw the juice in the microwave before adding it to the recipe.

Five-Spice Chicken Wings

3g CARB PER SERVING

PREP: 20 minutes **BAKE:** 20 minutes **SLOW COOK:** 3 to 4 hours (low) or 1½ to 2 hours (high)
MAKES: 32 servings (1 chicken piece and 1½ teaspoons sauce each)

1. Preheat oven to 375°F. Using a sharp knife, carefully cut off tips of the wings; discard wing tips. Cut each wing at joint to make two pieces.
2. In a foil-lined 15×10×1-inch baking pan arrange wing pieces in a single layer. Bake for 20 minutes. Drain well.
3. In a 3½- or 4-quart slow cooker combine plum sauce, butter, and five-spice powder. Add chicken pieces, stirring to coat with sauce.
4. Cover and cook on low-heat setting for 3 to 4 hours or on high-heat setting for 1½ to 2 hours.
5. Serve immediately or keep warm, covered, on warm-heat or low-heat setting for up to 1 hour. If desired, sprinkle with green onions.

16 **chicken wings (about 3 pounds)**
¾ **cup bottled plum sauce**
 1 **tablespoon butter, melted**
 1 **teaspoon five-spice powder**
   Slivered green onions (optional)

PER SERVING: 32 cal., 1 g total fat (0 g sat. fat), 9 mg chol., 45 mg sodium, 3 g carb. (0 g fiber, 2 g sugars), 3 g pro. Exchanges: 0.5 lean meat.

Chicken Kapama Bites

18g CARB PER SERVING

PREP: 20 minutes **SLOW COOK:** 6 to 7 hours (low) or 3 to 3½ hours (high)
MAKES: 12 servings (½ cup chicken mixture, 1 ounce [2 slices] bread, and 2 tablespoons arugula each)

Nonstick cooking spray
2½ pounds boneless, skinless chicken thighs, cut into bite-size pieces
1 large onion, halved and thinly sliced
¼ cup strong brewed coffee
¼ cup no-salt-added tomato paste
2 tablespoons honey or low-sugar apricot preserves
2 tablespoons balsamic vinegar
2 cloves garlic, minced
1 2-inch stick cinnamon
2 bay leaves
½ teaspoon black pepper
⅛ teaspoon ground cloves
12 ounces whole-wheat baguette, cut into 24 slices and toasted if desired
1½ cups baby arugula or baby spinach

1. Lightly coat an unheated very large skillet with cooking spray. Add chicken and onion, half at a time, and cook each portion for 3 to 4 minutes or until chicken is browned and onion is softened. Transfer to a 3½- or 4-quart slow cooker. In a medium bowl stir together coffee, tomato paste, honey, vinegar, garlic, cinnamon, bay leaves, pepper, and cloves. Pour over chicken in cooker.
2. Cover and cook on low-heat setting for 6 to 7 hours or on high-heat setting for 3 to 3½ hours. Serve chicken and onion on baguette slices and garnish with arugula.

PER SERVING: 207 cal., 5 g total fat (1 g sat. fat), 78 mg chol., 223 mg sodium, 18 g carb. (3 g fiber, 6 g sugars), 23 g pro. Exchanges: 1 starch, 3 lean meat.

Cook Well: Boneless chicken thighs and breasts are much easier to cut into bite-size pieces when you follow these tips:
- Place raw chicken in the freezer for about 30 minutes. This firms the meat, making it easier to work with.
- Use a sharp knife to slice the chicken crosswise into strips.
- Arrange the strips in a line and cut them again into chunks or cubes.

Barbecue Turkey Wedges

8g CARB PER SERVING

PREP: 15 minutes **SLOW COOK:** up to 2 hours (warm)
MAKES: 16 servings (2 pita wedges and 3 tablespoons turkey mixture each)

Nonstick cooking spray
1 pound lean ground turkey
¾ cup finely chopped red onion
3 cloves garlic, minced
1 14.5-ounce can no-salt-added diced tomatoes, undrained
⅓ cup bottled barbecue sauce
¼ teaspoon black pepper
½ of a small cucumber, seeded and chopped (½ cup)
1 recipe Pita Wedges

1. Coat a large unheated skillet with cooking spray. Cook turkey, ½ cup of the onion, and the garlic in skillet over medium-high heat for 5 to 8 minutes or until turkey is browned and onion is tender, stirring frequently. Drain fat.

2. Stir in tomatoes, barbecue sauce, and pepper; heat through. Transfer mixture to a 1½- or 2-quart slow cooker. Cover and keep warm on the warm-heat setting for up to 2 hours.

3. Just before serving, sprinkle turkey mixture in cooker with remaining chopped onion and cucumber. Serve turkey mixture with Pita Wedges.

Pita Wedges: Preheat oven to 350°F. Split two 6-inch whole wheat pita bread rounds in half horizontally. Cut each half into eight wedges. Arrange wedges in a single layer on a baking sheet. Bake for 10 to 15 minutes or until lightly browned and crisp; let cool.

PER SERVING: 80 cal., 2 g total fat (1 g sat. fat), 20 mg chol., 131 mg sodium, 8 g carb. (1 g fiber, 3 g sugars), 7 g pro. Exchanges: 0.5 starch, 1 lean meat.

Italian Cocktail Meatballs

3g CARB PER SERVING

PREP: 10 minutes **SLOW COOK:** 4 to 5 hours (low) or 2 to 2½ hours (high)
MAKES: 12 servings (1 meatball and about 1 tablespoon sauce each)

1. In a 1½- or 2-quart slow cooker combine meatballs and roasted sweet peppers. Sprinkle with crushed red pepper. Pour pasta sauce over all in cooker.
2. Cover and cook on low-heat setting for 4 to 5 hours or on high-heat setting for 2 to 2½ hours. If no heat setting is available, cook for 4 to 5 hours.
3. Skim fat from sauce. Stir meatballs gently before serving. Serve immediately or keep warm, covered, on warm-heat or low-heat setting (if available) for up to 2 hours. If desired, garnish with basil.

PER SERVING: 68 cal., 4 g total fat (1 g sat. fat), 30 mg chol., 182 mg sodium, 3 g carb. (0 g fiber, 1 g sugars), 6 g pro. Exchanges: 1 lean meat, 0.5 fat.

1 12-ounce package refrigerated or frozen cooked turkey meatballs, thawed (12)
½ cup bottled roasted red and/or yellow sweet peppers, drained and cut into 1-inch pieces
⅛ teaspoon crushed red pepper
1 cup bottled reduced-sodium pasta sauce
Snipped fresh basil (optional)

Tangy Cherry Barbecue Sausage

5 g
CARB PER SERVING

PREP: 15 minutes **SLOW COOK:** 4 hours (low)
MAKES: 36 servings (2 sausage pieces each)

1. In a 2-quart slow cooker combine onions, cherry preserves, tomato paste, vinegar, and chipotle chile pepper. Add sausage slices; toss to combine.
2. Cover and cook on low-heat setting for 4 hours. Serve immediately. Or keep warm on low-heat setting for up to 1 hour, stirring occasionally. Serve with toothpicks.

PER SERVING: 60 cal., 1 g total fat (0 g sat. fat), 16 mg chol., 227 mg sodium, 5 g carb. (0 g fiber, 3 g sugars), 4 g pro. Exchanges: 0.5 medium-fat meat.

2 **medium onions, finely chopped (1 cup)**
⅔ **cup cherry preserves**
¼ **cup no-salt-added tomato paste**
¼ **cup cider vinegar**
1 **teaspoon ground chipotle chile pepper**
2 **pounds cooked light smoked Polish sausage or smoked turkey sausage, cut into 72 slices (about ½ inch thick)**

Bourbon-Glazed Sausage Bites

7g CARB PER SERVING

PREP: 10 minutes **SLOW COOK:** 4 hours (low)
MAKES: 12 servings (2 sausage pieces each)

1 **pound cooked light smoked Polish sausage or smoked turkey sausage, cut into 1-inch slices**
⅓ **cup low-sugar apricot preserves**
3 **tablespoons pure maple syrup**
1 **tablespoon bourbon or water**
1 **teaspoon quick-cooking tapioca, crushed**

1. In a 1½-quart slow cooker combine sausage slices, apricot preserves, maple syrup, bourbon, and tapioca.

2. Cover and cook on low-heat setting for 4 hours. If no heat setting is available, cook for 4 hours.

3. Serve immediately or keep warm, covered, in the slow cooker for up to 1 hour. Serve with toothpicks.

PER SERVING: 86 cal., 2 g total fat (1 g sat. fat), 24 mg chol., 285 mg sodium, 7 g carb. (0 g fiber, 6 g sugars), 8 g pro. Exchanges: 0.5 carb., 1 lean meat.

Cook Well: Tapioca is a common thickener for sweet pies and puddings, but in the slow cooker the starch thickens savory liquids into delicate sauces. To prevent beads, crush tapioca with a mortar and pestle or place it in a resealable plastic bag and crush with a rolling pin.

Hoisin-Garlic Mushrooms

9 g
CARB PER
SERVING

PREP: 15 minutes **SLOW COOK:** 5 to 6 hours (low) or 2½ to 3 hours (high)
MAKES: 10 servings (¼ cup each)

1. In a 3½- or 4-quart slow cooker combine hoisin sauce, the water, garlic, and crushed red pepper. Add mushrooms, stirring to coat.
2. Cover and cook on low-heat setting for 5 to 6 hours or on high-heat setting for 2½ to 3 hours.
3. Using a slotted spoon, remove mushrooms from cooker. Discard cooking liquid. Serve warm mushrooms with appetizer picks.

PER SERVING: 43 cal., 1 g total fat (0 g sat. fat), 0 mg chol., 211 mg sodium, 9 g carb. (1 g fiber, 5 g sugars), 3 g pro. Exchanges: 0.5 carb, 0.5 vegetable.

½ cup bottled hoisin sauce
¼ cup water
2 tablespoons bottled minced garlic
¼ to ½ teaspoon crushed red pepper
24 ounces whole fresh button mushrooms, trimmed

Party Potatoes with Creamy Aïoli

24g CARB PER SERVING

PREP: 25 minutes **SLOW COOK:** 6 to 7 hours (low) or 3 to 3½ hours (high)
MAKES: 8 servings (about 4 potato pieces and 2 tablespoons aïoli each)

1. Coat an unheated 3½- or 4-quart slow cooker with cooking spray. Halve or quarter any large potatoes. Place potatoes and onion wedges in prepared cooker. In a small bowl stir together broth, 2 cloves garlic, and paprika. Pour over potatoes and onion in cooker.
2. Cover and cook on low-heat setting for 6 to 7 hours or on high-heat setting for 3 to 3½ hours. Place potato mixture in a serving bowl; toss with green onions, ¼ teaspoon salt, and pepper.
3. Meanwhile, for aïoli, in a small bowl whisk together sour cream, horseradish, chopped onion, dill, 2 cloves garlic, and ¼ teaspoon salt. Cover with plastic wrap; chill until serving time.
4. Serve potatoes warm or at room temperature with the aïoli.

PER SERVING: 132 cal., 3 g total fat (2 g sat. fat), 8 mg chol., 211 mg sodium, 24 g carb. (3 g fiber, 2 g sugars), 4 g pro. Exchanges: 1.5 starch, 0.5 fat.

Nonstick cooking spray
2 pounds tiny new potatoes
1 red onion, cut into thin wedges
½ cup reduced-sodium chicken broth
2 cloves garlic, minced
½ teaspoon smoked paprika or regular paprika
¼ cup finely chopped green onions (2)
¼ teaspoon salt
¼ teaspoon black pepper
1 8-ounce carton light sour cream
1 tablespoon prepared horseradish
1 tablespoon finely chopped onion
1 tablespoon snipped fresh dill or 1 teaspoon dried dill weed
2 cloves garlic, minced
¼ teaspoon salt

Ratatouille Dip

12g CARB PER SERVING

PREP: 35 minutes **SLOW COOK:** 1 hour (high), plus 30 minutes (low)
MAKES: 16 servings (¼ cup dip and ½ ounce bread each)

1 **14.5-ounce can crushed tomatoes**
1 **small eggplant, cubed**
1 **small zucchini, cubed**
1 **small yellow summer squash, cubed**
1 **small red sweet pepper, chopped**
1 **tablespoon fresh thyme leaves or 1 teaspoon dried thyme, crushed**
½ **teaspoon garlic powder**
½ **teaspoon black pepper**
½ **cup grated Parmesan cheese**
8 **ounces toasted baguette-style French bread slices or pita wedges**

1. In a 4-quart slow cooker stir together tomatoes, eggplant, zucchini, summer squash, and sweet pepper.
2. Cover and cook on high-heat setting for 1 hour. Stir in thyme, garlic powder, and black pepper. Turn to low-heat setting and cook for 30 minutes more.
3. Using a potato masher, crush the vegetable mixture to a chunky consistency. Stir in the Parmesan cheese. Stir occasionally while serving with baguette slices.

PER SERVING: 70 cal., 1 g total fat (1 g sat. fat), 2 mg chol., 146 mg sodium, 12 g carb. (2 g fiber, 2 g sugars), 4 g pro. Exchanges: 0.5 starch, 1 vegetable.

Cook Well: To toast French bread slices, place them in a single layer on a baking sheet. Broil 3 to 4 inches from heat for 2 to 3 minutes or until toasted, turning once.

Rio Grande Dip

12g CARB PER SERVING

PREP: 20 minutes **SLOW COOK:** 3 to 4 hours (low)
MAKES: 24 servings (2 tablespoons dip and about 6 chips each)

1. In a medium skillet crumble sausage and cook with onion over medium-high heat until meat is browned, stirring to break up sausage as it cooks. Drain off fat. Transfer meat mixture to a 1½-quart slow cooker. Stir in refried beans, the ¾ cup cheese, the salsa, and chiles.
2. Cover and cook on low-heat setting for 3 to 4 hours. If no heat setting is available, cook for 3 to 4 hours.
3. Stir well before serving. Serve immediately or keep warm, covered, on warm-heat or low-heat setting (if available) for up to 2 hours. If desired, sprinkle with the 2 tablespoons cheese. Serve dip with tortilla chips.

PER SERVING: 76 cal., 2 g total fat (1 g sat. fat), 5 mg chol., 258 mg sodium, 12 g carb. (2 g fiber, 1 g sugars), 4 g pro. Exchanges: 1 starch.

- 4 ounces uncooked Italian turkey sausage links, casings removed if needed
- ½ of a small onion, finely chopped
- 1 15-ounce can reduced-fat refried black beans
- ¾ cup shredded reduced-fat Monterey Jack cheese (3 ounces)
- ¾ cup bottled salsa
- ½ of a 4-ounce can diced green chiles, undrained
- 2 tablespoons shredded reduced-fat Monterey Jack cheese (optional)
- 1 9-ounce bag scoop-shape baked tortilla chips

Broccoli-Cheese Dip with Potato Dippers

12g CARB PER SERVING

PREP: 20 minutes SLOW COOK: 4 hours (low) or 2 hours (high)
MAKES: 16 servings (2 tablespoons dip and 4 Potato Dippers each)

1 8-ounce package reduced-fat cream cheese (Neufchâtel), cut up
6 ounces reduced-fat pasteurized prepared cheese product
1½ cups broccoli, blanched* and chopped
3 tablespoons bottled salsa
4 teaspoons bacon-flavor vegetable protein bits
   Fat-free milk (optional)
1 recipe Potato Dippers

1. In a 1½- or 2-quart slow cooker combine cream cheese, cheese product, broccoli, salsa, and bacon-flavor bits.
2. Cover and cook on low-heat setting for 4 hours or on high-heat setting for 2 hours. If no heat setting is available, cook for 3 hours.
3. Stir dip before serving. If desired, thin dip to desired consistency with milk. Serve with Potato Dippers.

Potato Dippers: Scrub 4 medium russet potatoes; cut each potato into 16 slices. Place potato slices in a large bowl and add enough cold water to cover. Let stand for 10 minutes. Preheat oven to 450°F. Lightly coat a large baking sheet with nonstick cooking spray. Drain potatoes and pat dry with paper towels. Place potatoes in an even layer on the prepared baking sheet. Lightly coat potato slices with cooking spray. Sprinkle with 1 teaspoon chili powder and ½ teaspoon black pepper. Bake potatoes about 25 minutes or until lightly browned and slightly crisp.

*Test Kitchen Tip: To blanch broccoli, place it in a pot of boiling water; cook for 4 to 5 minutes. Remove broccoli with a slotted spoon and plunge into a bowl of ice water; drain and chop.

PER SERVING: 108 cal., 4 g total fat (3 g sat. fat), 14 mg chol., 256 mg sodium, 12 g carb. (1 g fiber, 2 g sugars), 5 g pro. Exchanges: 1 starch, 1 fat.

On the Side: Color up your party tray with fresh vegetables alongside the dips and spreads. Here's how to prep veggies for optimum dipping action:
- **Sweet peppers:** Offer various colors; slice at least 1 inch thick.
- **Broccoli:** Separate into florets. Plunge the florets into boiling water briefly, then into ice water to boost their flavor, color, and crispness.
- **Jicama:** Peel and slice into ½-inch strips.
- **Cherry tomatoes:** Serve whole with toothpicks.
- **Romaine lettuce:** Use the interior leaves, which make crunchy scoops.
- **Asparagus:** Trim woody bases. Plunge the spears into boiling water, then into ice water to keep them colorful and crunchy.
- **Baby radishes:** Serve sliced. They'll add a spicy bite to the table.
- **Carrots and celery:** Serve these workhorse dippers sliced into thin sticks.

White Bean Spread

13g
CARB PER
SERVING

PREP: 15 minutes **SLOW COOK:** 3 to 4 hours (low)
MAKES: 20 servings (2 tablespoons dip and 2 to 3 chips each)

2 15-ounce cans great northern or white kidney beans (cannellini beans), rinsed and drained
½ cup reduced-sodium chicken or vegetable broth
1 tablespoon olive oil
3 cloves garlic, minced
1 teaspoon snipped fresh marjoram or ¼ teaspoon dried marjoram, crushed
½ teaspoon snipped fresh rosemary or ⅛ teaspoon dried rosemary, crushed
⅛ teaspoon black pepper
Fresh marjoram and rosemary (optional)
1 recipe Whole Wheat Pita Chips

1. In a 1½-quart slow cooker combine beans, broth, oil, garlic, marjoram, rosemary, and pepper.
2. Cover and cook on low-heat setting for 3 to 4 hours. If no heat setting is available, cook for 3 to 4 hours.
3. Using a potato masher, slightly mash bean mixture. Spoon bean mixture into a serving bowl. If desired, sprinkle with additional fresh marjoram and rosemary. Serve dip warm or at room temperature with Whole Wheat Pita Chips.

Whole Wheat Pita Chips: Preheat oven to 350°F. Split 4 whole wheat pita bread rounds horizontally in half; cut each circle into six wedges. Place pita wedges in a single layer on large baking sheets. In a small bowl combine 2 tablespoons olive oil, 2 teaspoons snipped fresh oregano, and ¼ teaspoon kosher salt; brush pita wedges very lightly with oil mixture. Bake for 12 to 15 minutes or until crisp and lightly browned. Remove from baking sheet; cool on a wire rack.

Make-Ahead Directions: Cook and mash bean mixture as directed. Transfer bean mixture to an airtight container; seal. Chill for up to 24 hours. Bring bean mixture to room temperature before serving.

PER SERVING: 77 cal., 2 g total fat (0 g sat. fat), 0 mg chol., 173 mg sodium, 13 g carb. (3 g fiber, 0 g sugars), 4 g pro. Exchanges: 1 starch, 0.5 lean meat.

Fruit Chutney with Spiced Chips

21g CARB PER SERVING

PREP: 25 minutes **SLOW COOK:** 2 hours (high)
MAKES: 24 servings (2 tablespoons chutney, 3 chips, and 1 teaspoon cheese each)

1. For chutney, in a 3½- or 4-quart slow cooker combine apples, pears, onion, cranberries, brown sugar, vinegar, cinnamon, ginger, and salt.
2. Cover and cook on high-heat setting for 1 hour. In a small bowl combine cornstarch and the cold water; stir into cooker. Cover and cook on high-heat setting for 1 hour more.
3. Serve chutney warm or at room temperature with Spiced Chips and top each serving with crumbled goat cheese.

Spiced Chips: Preheat oven to 400°F. Using a pizza wheel, cut 9 whole wheat tortillas each into eight wedges. Place tortilla wedges in a single layer on baking sheets. Lightly coat wedges with nonstick cooking spray. Mix together ½ teaspoon granulated sugar** and ¼ teaspoon ground coriander. Sprinkle evenly over tortilla wedges. Bake for 10 minutes, turning once halfway through baking.

***Sugar Substitutes:** Choose from Sweet'N Low Brown or Sugar Twin Granulated Brown. Follow package directions to use product amount equivalent to ⅓ cup brown sugar.

****Sugar Substitute:** We do not recommend using a sugar substitute for the chips.

PER SERVING: 114 cal., 2 g total fat (1 g sat. fat), 4 mg chol., 182 mg sodium, 21 g carb. (2 g fiber, 9 g sugars), 3 g pro. Exchanges: 1 starch, 0.5 carb., 0.5 fat.

PER SERVING WITH SUBSTITUTE: Same as above, except, 102 cal., 181 mg sodium, 18 g carb. (7 g sugars). Exchanges: 0 carb.

2 large apples, such as Braeburn, cored and cut into 1-inch pieces
2 large pears, such as Anjou, cored and cut into 1-inch pieces
1 small sweet onion, chopped
1 cup fresh or frozen whole cranberries, thawed
⅓ cup packed brown sugar*
¼ cup balsamic vinegar
1 teaspoon ground cinnamon
1 teaspoon ground ginger
⅛ teaspoon salt
1 tablespoon cornstarch
2 tablespoons cold water
1 recipe Spiced Chips
4 ounces goat cheese (chèvre), crumbled

Cook Well: Onions that contain smaller amounts of sulfur, such as Maui, Vidalia, and Walla Walla, tend to taste sweeter. Because of their mildness, they work well when served raw in salads and relishes but also add a pleasantly sweet flavor when cooked.

Sweet onions are more perishable than regular onions. Buy only the amount you need and store for just a week or two at room temperature.

Chocolate Fondue with Fruit Kabobs

21g CARB PER SERVING

PREP: 20 minutes **SLOW COOK:** 30 to 45 minutes (low)
MAKES: 16 servings (2 tablespoons chocolate mixture and 1 fruit kabob each)

1. In a 1½- or 2-quart slow cooker combine whipped topping and chocolate pieces. Cover and cook on low-heat setting for 30 to 45 minutes, stirring once or twice during cooking time (whipped topping will deflate).
2. To assemble the fruit kabobs, on each skewer place about 6 pieces of fruit; set aside.
3. When chocolate is completely melted, whisk in coffee, 1 tablespoon at a time, until desired consistency (thick but pourable). To serve, keep warm on warm-heat setting. If necessary, add additional coffee to thin the chocolate mixture. Serve with fruit kabobs.

PER SERVING: 159 cal., 7 g total fat (5 g sat. fat), 1 mg chol., 4 mg sodium, 21 g carb. (3 g fiber, 15 g sugars), 1 g pro. Exchanges: 1 carb., 0.5 fruit, 1.5 fat.

1 8-ounce container frozen light whipped dessert topping, thawed
1 10- to 12-ounce package dark chocolate pieces
16 6-inch wooden skewers
64 fresh strawberry halves, fresh pineapple chunks, apple chunks, and/or kiwifruit chunks
1 pint fresh raspberries
¼ cup hot strong coffee

Barbecue Snack Mix

12g CARB PER SERVING

PREP: 10 minutes **SLOW COOK:** 2 hours (low) or 1 hour (high) **COOL:** 30 minutes
MAKES: 24 servings (⅓ cup each)

Nonstick cooking spray
3 cups crispy corn and rice cereal
2 cups bite-size multibran cereal
2 cups oyster crackers
⅔ cup slivered almonds
1 teaspoon dried thyme leaves, crushed
1 teaspoon paprika
1 teaspoon packed brown sugar*
¼ teaspoon ground cumin
¼ teaspoon dry mustard
⅛ teaspoon cayenne pepper
3 tablespoons olive oil

1. Lightly coat an unheated 5- to 6-quart slow cooker with cooking spray. In prepared slow cooker combine cereals, crackers, and almonds. In a small bowl stir together the thyme, paprika, brown sugar, cumin, mustard, and cayenne. Drizzle cereal mixture with oil, tossing gently to blend. Sprinkle with spice mixture, tossing gently to coat.

2. Cover and cook on low-heat setting for 2 hours, stirring every 30 minutes, or on high-heat setting for 1 hour, stirring every 20 minutes.

3. Spread mixture in an even layer on a 13×9×2-inch baking pan; cool completely. Store in an airtight container for up to 2 weeks.

*Sugar Substitutes: Choose from Sweet'N Low Brown or Sugar Twin Granulated Brown. Follow package directions to use product amount equivalent to 1 teaspoon brown sugar.

PER SERVING: 81 cal., 4 g total fat (0 g sat. fat), 0 mg chol., 115 mg sodium, 12 g carb. (1 g fiber, 2 g sugars), 1 g pro. Exchanges: 1 starch, 0.5 fat.

PER SERVING WITH SUBSTITUTE: Same as above, except 80 cal.

Lemon-Zested Snack Mix

16g
CARB PER SERVING

PREP: 15 minutes **SLOW COOK:** 2½ hours (low) or 1 hour 20 minutes (high)
MAKES: 24 servings (⅓ cup each)

Nonstick cooking spray
5 cups **bite-size multigrain or wheat square cereal**
2 cups **plain pita chips, broken into bite-size pieces**
⅔ cup **chopped walnuts**
¼ cup **pumpkin seeds (pepitas)**
1 **1-ounce packet dry ranch salad dressing mix**
2 teaspoons **dried dill weed**
1 teaspoon **dried rosemary, crushed**
2 tablespoons **olive oil**
1 tablespoon **finely shredded lemon peel**

1. Lightly coat an unheated 5- to 6-quart slow cooker with cooking spray. In prepared slow cooker combine cereal, pita chips, walnuts, pumpkin seeds, salad dressing mix, dill weed, and rosemary. Drizzle mixture with oil, tossing gently to blend.
2. Cover and cook on low-heat setting for 2½ hours (stir every 40 minutes) or on high-heat setting for 1 hour 20 minutes (stir every 20 minutes).
3. Sprinkle lemon peel over mixture, tossing gently to blend. Spread mixture in an even layer on a 13×9×2-inch baking sheet; cool completely. Store in an airtight container for up to 2 weeks.

PER SERVING: 113 cal., 5 g total fat (1 g sat. fat), 0 mg chol., 220 mg sodium, 16 g carb. (2 g fiber, 3 g sugars), 3 g pro. Exchanges: 1 starch, 1 fat.

Bourbon-Citrus Sipper

12g CARB PER SERVING

PREP: 15 minutes **SLOW COOK:** 3½ to 4 hours (low) or 2 hours (high), plus 30 minutes (low or high)
MAKES: 8 servings (¾ cup each)

1. In a 3- or 3½-quart slow cooker combine apple cider, sugar (if using), cinnamon, cloves, and anise seeds.
2. Cover and cook on low-heat setting for 3½ to 4 hours or on high-heat setting for 2 hours. Add orange slices and lemon slices. Cover and cook for 30 minutes more.
3. Place a fine-mesh sieve over a large bowl; strain cider mixture. If using high-heat setting, turn cooker to low-heat setting. Pour the strained mixture back into the slow cooker to keep warm.
4. Just before serving, add bourbon and sugar substitute (if using) to cider mixture.

*Sugar Substitutes: Choose from Splenda Granular or Sweet'N Low bulk or packets. Follow package directions to use product amount equivalent to ¼ cup sugar. Add sugar substitute just before serving.

PER SERVING: 141 cal., 0 g total fat, 0 mg chol., 1 mg sodium, 12 g carb. (1 g fiber, 9 g sugars),1 g pro. Exchanges: 0.5 carb., 0.5 fruit.

PER SERVING WITH SUBSTITUTE: Same as above, except 120 cal., 7 g carb. (3 g sugars). Exchanges: 0 carb.

6 **cups apple cider or apple juice (48 ounces)**
¼ **cup sugar***
9 **inches stick cinnamon**
8 **whole cloves**
¼ **teaspoon anise seeds**
1 **large navel orange, sliced**
1 **medium lemon, sliced**
½ **cup bourbon**

comforting favorites

Braising pot roasts, pork chops, meaty poultry, and other robust cuts in your slow cooker makes them taste rich and bold. And thanks to trimmed-down recipes that keep fat and calories in check, these and other mealtime classics are better for you, too.

Simple Hoisin Chicken

31g CARB PER SERVING

PREP: 15 minutes **SLOW COOK:** 4 to 5 hours (low) or 2½ hours (high), plus 30 to 45 minutes (high)
MAKES: 6 servings (2 chicken thighs, ½ cup vegetable mixture, and ⅓ cup rice each)

Nonstick cooking spray
12 bone-in chicken thighs
(3½ to 4 pounds total),
skinned
2 tablespoons quick-cooking
tapioca
⅛ teaspoon salt
⅛ teaspoon black pepper
½ cup bottled hoisin sauce
1 16-ounce package frozen
broccoli stir-fry vegetables
2 cups hot cooked
brown rice

1. Coat an unheated 3½- or 4-quart slow cooker with cooking spray. Place chicken in the prepared cooker. Sprinkle chicken with tapioca, salt, and pepper. Pour hoisin sauce over chicken.
2. Cover and cook on low-heat setting for 4 to 5 hours or on high-heat setting for 2½ hours.
3. If using low-heat setting, turn to high-heat setting. Stir in frozen vegetables. Cover and cook for 30 to 45 minutes more or just until vegetables are tender. Serve over hot cooked rice.

PER SERVING: 332 cal., 7 g total fat (2 g sat. fat), 126 mg chol., 524 mg sodium, 31 g carb. (3 g fiber, 8 g sugars), 34 g pro. Exchanges: 1.5 starch, 4 lean meat, 1 vegetable, 0.5 fat.

Time-Saving Trick: Time-pressed cooks love frozen vegetables—no peeling or slicing needed. In most cases, you can skip the thawing step; unless otherwise specified, frozen vegetables should be added to the slow cooker directly from the freezer. Because they are frozen at their peak, frozen vegetables are often just as nutritious as fresh.

Country Captain

34g CARB PER SERVING

PREP: 25 minutes **SLOW COOK:** 5 to 6 hours (low) or 2½ to 3 hours (high)
MAKES: 6 servings (2 chicken pieces, ½ cup vegetables, and ⅓ cup rice each)

1 medium sweet onion (such as Vidalia, Maui, or Walla Walla), cut into thin wedges
12 small chicken drumsticks and/or thighs (about 3 pounds total), skinned
2 medium green and/or yellow sweet peppers, cut into thin strips
¼ cup currants or golden raisins
2 cloves garlic, minced
1 14.5-ounce can diced tomatoes, undrained
2 tablespoons quick-cooking tapioca, crushed
2 to 3 teaspoons curry powder
½ teaspoon ground cumin
¼ teaspoon ground mace
¼ teaspoon salt
2 cups hot cooked white or brown rice
2 tablespoons chopped green onion (1)
2 tablespoons sliced almonds, toasted

1. In a 3½- or 4-quart slow cooker place onion, chicken, sweet peppers, currants, and garlic. In a large bowl combine tomatoes, tapioca, curry powder, cumin, mace, and salt. Pour over all in cooker.
2. Cover and cook on low-heat setting for 5 to 6 hours or on high-heat setting for 2½ to 3 hours.
3. Serve chicken mixture over rice. Sprinkle with green onion and almonds.

PER SERVING: 283 cal., 6 g total fat (1 g sat. fat), 80 mg chol., 509 mg sodium, 34 g carb. (3 g fiber, 10 g sugars), 24 g pro. Exchanges: 2 starch, 2.5 lean meat, 1 vegetable.

Garlic Chicken with Artichokes

32g CARB PER SERVING

PREP: 20 minutes **SLOW COOK:** 5 hours (low) or 2½ hours (high), plus 30 to 60 minutes (high)
MAKES: 8 servings (1 cup chicken mixture and ½ cup rice each)

1. In a 3½- or 4-quart slow cooker combine sweet peppers, onions, garlic, tapioca, rosemary, lemon peel, and black pepper. Pour broth over mixture in cooker. Add chicken.
2. Cover and cook on low-heat setting for 5 hours or on high-heat setting for 2½ hours.
3. If using low-heat setting, turn to high-heat setting. Stir in frozen artichoke hearts and lemon juice. Cover and cook for 30 to 60 minutes more. Serve with rice and, if desired, lemon wedges and rosemary sprigs.

PER SERVING: 358 cal., 8 g total fat (2 g sat. fat), 141 mg chol., 233 mg sodium, 32 g carb. (5 g fiber, 3 g sugars), 38 g pro. Exchanges: 2 starch, 3 lean meat, 2 vegetable, 0.5 fat.

- 2 **medium red sweet peppers, cut into 1-inch-wide strips**
- 2 **medium onions, cut into wedges**
- 12 **cloves garlic, peeled**
- 1 **tablespoon quick-cooking tapioca**
- 2 **teaspoons dried rosemary, crushed**
- 1 **teaspoon finely shredded lemon peel**
- ½ **teaspoon black pepper**
- ½ **cup chicken broth**
- 3 **pounds skinless, boneless chicken thighs**
- 1 **8- to 9-ounce package frozen artichoke hearts**
- 1 **tablespoon lemon juice**
- 4 **cups hot cooked brown rice**
  Lemon wedges (optional)
  Rosemary sprigs (optional)

Cajun Chicken with Okra

PREP: 20 minutes **SLOW COOK:** 6 to 7 hours (low) or 3 to 3½ hours (high)
MAKES: 4 servings (2 drumsticks, 1¼ cups vegetable mixture, and ½ cup rice each)

1. Coat an unheated 6-quart slow cooker with cooking spray. Combine the sweet peppers, onion, okra, and celery in the prepared cooker. Top with chicken. Sprinkle chicken with paprika, thyme, and salt. Top with tomatoes. In a small bowl combine the broth and 1 tablespoon pepper sauce. Pour over all in cooker.
2. Cover and cook on low-heat setting for 6 to 7 hours or on high-heat setting for 3 to 3½ hours. Serve chicken and vegetable mixture over rice in shallow bowls. If desired, pass additional pepper sauce.

PER SERVING: 408 cal., 8 g total fat (2 g sat. fat), 157 mg chol., 563 mg sodium, 35 g carb. (5 g fiber, 6 g sugars), 47 g pro. Exchanges: 2 starch, 5 lean meat, 1 vegetable.

Nonstick cooking spray
2 medium green sweet peppers, cut into 1-inch pieces
1 medium red sweet pepper, cut into 1-inch pieces
1 large onion, chopped (1 cup)
1 cup fresh or frozen sliced okra
1 stalk celery, sliced (½ cup)
8 chicken drumsticks, skinned
2 teaspoons smoked paprika
1 teaspoon dried thyme, crushed
¼ teaspoon salt
1 cup grape tomatoes
¼ cup reduced-sodium chicken broth
1 tablespoon bottled cayenne pepper sauce
2 cups hot cooked brown rice
Bottled cayenne pepper sauce (optional)

Chicken and Shrimp Paella

36g CARB PER SERVING

PREP: 25 minutes **SLOW COOK:** 8 to 10 hours (low) or 4 to 5 hours (high), plus 30 to 45 minutes (high)
STAND: 10 minutes **MAKES:** 10 servings (1⅓ cups each)

1 medium green sweet pepper, chopped (¾ cup)

1 medium onion, chopped (½ cup)

2 cloves garlic, minced

3 medium tomatoes, chopped (1½ cups)

2 cups reduced-sodium chicken broth

1 cup water

2 teaspoons dried oregano, crushed

½ teaspoon salt

½ teaspoon ground turmeric

½ teaspoon black pepper

½ teaspoon bottled hot pepper sauce (optional)

3 pounds chicken thighs and drumsticks, skinned

8 ounces smoked turkey sausage link, halved lengthwise and sliced

2 cups uncooked long grain rice

8 ounces cooked, peeled, and deveined shrimp (tails removed), thawed if frozen

1 cup frozen peas

1. In a 6-quart slow cooker combine sweet pepper, onion, garlic, tomatoes, broth, the water, oregano, salt, turmeric, black pepper, and, if desired, hot pepper sauce. Top with chicken and sausage.

2. Cover and cook on low-heat setting for 8 to 10 hours or on high-heat setting for 4 to 5 hours.

3. Stir in rice. If using low-heat setting, turn to high-heat setting. Cover and cook for 30 to 45 minutes more or until rice is tender. If desired, remove chicken from cooker. Pull the chicken from the bones. Return chicken to cooker along with the shrimp and peas. Cover and let stand for 10 minutes.

PER SERVING: 312 cal., 5 g total fat (1 g sat. fat), 121 mg chol., 568 mg sodium, 36 g carb. (2 g fiber, 3 g sugars) 28 g pro. Exchanges: 2 starch, 3 lean meat, 1 vegetable.

Greek Braised Chicken Legs

32g CARB PER SERVING

PREP: 25 minutes SLOW COOK: 6 to 8 hours (low) or 3 to 4 hours (high)
MAKES: 4 servings (2 drumsticks and ½ cup brown rice each)

1. Place onion in a 3½- or 4-quart slow cooker. Sprinkle drumsticks with Greek seasoning. Place drumsticks on top of onion in cooker. Top drumsticks with tomatoes, olives, and garlic.
2. Cover and cook on low-heat setting for 6 to 8 hours or on high-heat setting for 3 to 4 hours.
3. Using a slotted spoon, serve chicken mixture over hot cooked brown rice. If desired, spoon some of the cooking liquid over top. Sprinkle with parsley and lemon peel.

PER SERVING: 404 cal., 9 g total fat (2 g sat. fat), 157 mg chol., 338 mg sodium, 32 g carb. (4 g fiber, 5 g sugars), 46 g pro. Exchanges: 1.5 starch, 5.5 lean meat, 1 vegetable.

- 1 medium onion, sliced
- 8 chicken drumsticks (about 2¾ pounds total), skinned
- 1 teaspoon Greek seasoning
- 3 cups halved grape tomatoes or cherry tomatoes
- ¼ cup chopped pimiento-stuffed green olives
- 4 cloves garlic, minced
- 2 cups hot cooked brown rice
- ¼ cup snipped fresh parsley or parsley sprigs
- 1 teaspoon finely shredded lemon peel

Cook Well: To easily remove the skin from a chicken drumstick, hold the meaty end and pull the skin down with a paper towel.

Jamaican Jerk Chicken

41g CARB PER SERVING

PREP: 25 minutes **SLOW COOK:** 5 to 5½ hours (low) or 2½ to 2¾ hours (high)
MAKES: 8 servings (¾ cup chicken mixture and ⅓ cup cooked rice each)

1 **20-ounce can pineapple chunks (juice pack)**
1¾ **pounds skinless, boneless chicken thighs, cut into 1-inch pieces**
1 **15-ounce can black beans, rinsed and drained**
1 **small fresh jalapeño chile pepper, seeded and finely chopped***
6 **tablespoons finely chopped green onions (3)**
2 **tablespoons quick-cooking tapioca, crushed**
2 **tablespoons red wine vinegar**
1 **tablespoon Dijon-style mustard**
4 **to 6 teaspoons salt-free jerk seasoning**
½ **teaspoon salt**
¼ **teaspoon black pepper**
1 **orange, peeled and sectioned**
2 **cups hot cooked brown rice**
  Sliced green onions (optional)

1. Drain pineapple, reserving juice. In a 3½- or 4-quart slow cooker place chicken, pineapple chunks, beans, jalapeño pepper, and chopped green onions.
2. In a small bowl combine reserved pineapple juice, tapioca, vinegar, mustard, jerk seasoning, salt, and black pepper; pour into cooker.
3. Cover and cook on low-heat setting for 5 to 5½ hours or on high-heat setting for 2½ to 2¾ hours.
4. To serve, top with orange sections. Serve with hot cooked rice and, if desired, sprinkle with sliced green onions.

*Test Kitchen Tip: Because chile peppers contain volatile oils that can burn your skin and eyes, avoid direct contact with them as much as possible. When working with chile peppers, wear plastic or rubber gloves. If your bare hands do touch the peppers, wash your hands and nails well with soap and warm water.

PER SERVING: 300 cal., 5 g total fat (1 g sat. fat), 82 mg chol., 449 mg sodium, 41 g carb. (6 g fiber, 12 g sugars), 27 g pro. Exchanges: 2 starch, 0.5 fruit, 3 lean meat.

Sesame Turkey

PREP: 15 minutes **SLOW COOK:** 5 to 6 hours (low) or 2½ to 3 hours (high)
MAKES: 8 servings (4 ounces meat and about 3 tablespoons sauce each)

1. Place turkey in a 3½- or 4-quart slow cooker. Sprinkle with black pepper and cayenne pepper. In a small bowl combine broth, soy sauce, ginger, lemon juice, sesame oil, and garlic. Pour over turkey in cooker.
2. Cover and cook on low-heat setting for 5 to 6 hours or on high-heat setting for 2½ to 3 hours.
3. Transfer turkey to a serving platter, reserving cooking liquid. Cover turkey to keep warm.
4. For sauce, strain cooking liquid into a small saucepan. In a small bowl combine cornstarch and the cold water. Stir into liquid in saucepan. Cook and stir over medium heat until thickened and bubbly; cook and stir for 2 minutes more. Slice turkey. Spoon sauce over turkey and sprinkle with green onion slivers and sesame seeds.

PER SERVING: 222 cal., 3 g total fat (1 g sat. fat), 112 mg chol., 373 mg sodium, 3 g carb. (0 g fiber, 0 g sugars), 42 g pro. Exchanges: 6 lean meat.

- 3 pounds turkey breast tenderloins
- ¼ teaspoon black pepper
- ⅛ teaspoon cayenne pepper
- ¼ cup reduced-sodium chicken broth
- ¼ cup reduced-sodium soy sauce
- 4 teaspoons grated fresh ginger
- 1 tablespoon lemon juice
- 1 tablespoon toasted sesame oil
- 2 cloves garlic, minced
- 2 tablespoons cornstarch
- 2 tablespoons cold water
- 2 tablespoons green onion slivers
- 1 tablespoon sesame seeds, toasted

Smoked Turkey and Bulgur

17g CARB PER SERVING

PREP: 20 minutes **SLOW COOK:** 3 hours (low)
MAKES: 8 servings (1 cup each)

Nonstick cooking spray
1 large onion, chopped (1 cup)
1 medium green sweet pepper, cut into 1-inch pieces (1 cup)
1 stalk celery, sliced (½ cup)
1½ cups water
1 medium smoked turkey drumstick, skin and bone removed and meat chopped (about 4 cups)
1 cup uncooked bulgur
¼ teaspoon black pepper
1 medium zucchini, coarsely chopped (1½ cups)
1 tablespoon snipped fresh sage

1. Coat an unheated 4-quart slow cooker with cooking spray. Place onion, sweet pepper, and celery in the cooker. Stir in the water, turkey, bulgur, and black pepper.
2. Cover and cook on low-heat setting for 2½ hours. Stir in zucchini and sage. Cover and cook for 30 minutes more.

PER SERVING: 216 cal., 7 g total fat (2 g sat. fat), 57 mg chol., 684 mg sodium, 17 g carb. (4 g fiber, 2 g sugars), 22 g pro. Exchanges: 1 starch, 2.5 lean meat, 0.5 vegetable, 0.5 fat.

Time-Saving Trick: If you use onions often and want them ready in a flash, try frozen chopped onions. Return unused frozen onions to the freezer. If you have more fresh chopped onions than you need, store them in a sealed container in the refrigerator for up to 1 week.

Pork Tenderloin with Sweet-Spiced Onions

33g CARB PER SERVING

PREP: 25 minutes **SLOW COOK:** 2 hours (low) or 1½ hours (high), plus 15 minutes (high)
MAKES: 4 servings (3 ounces meat, ½ cup couscous mixture, and ¼ cup sauce each)

½ teaspoon coarsely ground black pepper
½ teaspoon ground cinnamon
¼ teaspoon ground allspice
⅛ teaspoon salt
1 pound pork tenderloin
2 teaspoons canola oil
Nonstick cooking spray
1 large onion, chopped (1 cup)
½ teaspoon finely shredded orange peel (set aside)
¼ cup orange juice
2 tablespoons reduced-sodium soy sauce
2 teaspoons cornstarch
2 teaspoons sugar*
2 cups hot cooked whole wheat couscous
½ cup frozen peas, thawed
1 ounce sliced almonds, toasted (about ¼ cup)

1. In a small bowl combine pepper, cinnamon, allspice, and salt. Sprinkle evenly over the pork and press onto meat.
2. In a large nonstick skillet heat 1 teaspoon of the oil over medium-high heat. Brown pork in hot oil about 4 minutes, turning occasionally to brown evenly. Lightly coat an unheated 3- or 3½-quart slow cooker with cooking spray. Place pork in cooker. Heat the remaining 1 teaspoon oil in the skillet. Cook onion in skillet about 4 minutes or until browned, stirring frequently. Spoon onion around pork in the slow cooker. Pour orange juice over onion.
3. Cover and cook on low-heat setting for 2 hours or on high-heat setting for 1½ hours or until internal temperature of pork registers 150°F on an instant-read thermometer.
4. Transfer pork to a cutting board; cover to keep warm. If using low-heat setting, turn to high-heat setting. In a small bowl whisk together soy sauce, cornstarch, sugar, and reserved orange peel until cornstarch is completely dissolved. Stir into onion mixture in slow cooker. Cover and cook for 15 minutes more to thicken slightly.
5. To serve, toss couscous with peas and almonds. Slice pork and serve with couscous mixture and sauce.

*Sugar Substitutes: Choose from Splenda Granular or Sweet'N Low bulk or packets. Follow package directions to use product amount equivalent to 2 teaspoons sugar.

PER SERVING: 340 cal., 10 g total fat (2 g sat. fat), 71 mg chol., 408 mg sodium, 33 g carb. (4 g fiber, 7 g sugars), 29 g pro. Exchanges: 2 starch, 3.5 lean meat.

PER SERVING WITH SUBSTITUTE: Same as above, except 333 cal., 31 g carb. (6 g sugars).

Sweet-and-Sour Pork

40g CARB PER SERVING

PREP: 30 minutes **SLOW COOK:** 7 to 8 hours (low) or 3½ to 4 hours (high)
MAKES: 8 servings (1 cup pork mixture and ⅓ cup rice each)

1 **20-ounce can pineapple chunks (juice pack)**
2 **medium carrots, bias sliced (1 cup)**
1 **large onion, cut into thin wedges**
1 **8-ounce can sliced water chestnuts, drained**
1 **medium red sweet pepper, cut into 1-inch pieces**
1 **stalk celery, bias sliced (½ cup)**
2 **pounds boneless pork shoulder roast, trimmed of fat and cut into 1-inch pieces**
2 **tablespoons packed brown sugar***
2 **tablespoons rice vinegar**
2 **tablespoons tomato paste**
2 **tablespoons quick-cooking tapioca, crushed**
1 **tablespoon reduced-sodium soy sauce**
2 **cloves garlic, minced**
½ **teaspoon toasted sesame oil**
3 **cups hot cooked brown rice**
½ **cup chopped green onions (4) (optional)**

1. Drain pineapple chunks, reserving ⅓ cup of the juice; set pineapple chunks aside.
2. In a 3½- or 4-quart slow cooker combine carrots, onion, water chestnuts, sweet pepper, and celery. Top with pork. In a medium bowl whisk together reserved ⅓ cup pineapple juice, the brown sugar (if using), rice vinegar, tomato paste, tapioca, soy sauce, garlic, and sesame oil. Pour over all in cooker.
3. Cover and cook on low-heat setting for 7 to 8 hours or on high-heat setting for 3½ to 4 hours. Skim fat if needed.
4. Stir in reserved pineapple chunks and sugar substitute (if using). Serve over hot cooked rice. If desired, sprinkle with green onions.

*Sugar Substitutes: Choose from Sweet'N Low Brown or Sugar Twin Granulated Brown. Follow package directions to use product amount equivalent to 2 tablespoons brown sugar. Stir in sugar substitute after cooking.

PER SERVING: 338 cal., 8 g total fat (3 g sat. fat), 73 mg chol., 223 mg sodium, 40 g carb. (4 g fiber, 15 g sugars), 25 g pro. Exchanges: 2 starch, 0.5 fruit, 2.5 lean meat, 1 vegetable, 0.5 fat.

PER SERVING WITH SUBSTITUTE: Same as above, except: 325 cal., 222 mg sodium, 37 g carb. (12 g sugars).

Cranberry-Chipotle Country-Style Ribs

PREP: 15 minutes SLOW COOK: 7 to 8 hours (low) or 3½ to 4 hours (high)
MAKES: 8 servings (4 ounces cooked meat and ¼ cup sauce each)

24g CARB PER SERVING

1. Trim fat from ribs. Sprinkle ribs with the salt and black pepper. Place ribs in a 3½- or 4-quart slow cooker. In a medium bowl combine cranberry sauce, onion, chipotle peppers, and garlic; pour over ribs in cooker.
2. Cover and cook on low-heat setting for 7 to 8 hours or on high-heat setting for 3½ to 4 hours.
3. Transfer ribs to a serving platter. Stir sauce. Drizzle some of the sauce over ribs. If desired, serve with the remaining sauce and/or steamed green beans.

*Test Kitchen Tip: Because chile peppers contain volatile oils that can burn your skin and eyes, avoid direct contact with them as much as possible. When working with chile peppers, wear plastic or rubber gloves. If your bare hands do touch the peppers, wash your hands and nails well with soap and warm water.

2½ to 3 pounds boneless pork country-style ribs
¼ teaspoon salt
¼ teaspoon black pepper
1 16-ounce can whole cranberry sauce
1 large onion, chopped (1 cup)
3 chipotle peppers in adobo sauce, finely chopped*
1½ teaspoons bottled minced garlic (3 cloves)
Steamed green beans (optional)

PER SERVING: 270 cal., 10 g total fat (2 g sat. fat), 68 mg chol., 149 mg sodium, 24 g carb. (0 g fiber, 19 g sugars), 18 g pro. Exchanges: 1.5 carb., 2.5 medium-fat meat.

Cook Well: Chipotle peppers are dried smoked jalapeño peppers. They're often found canned in adobo, a dark red Mexican sauce made from ground chiles, herbs, and vinegar.

Many recipes call for one, two, or just a few chipotle peppers. You can freeze leftover chipotle peppers. Pack them, covered with the adobo sauce from the can, in a freezer container. Seal, label, and freeze for up to 2 months. When needed, thaw in the refrigerator or defrost in the microwave.

Braised Pork with Salsa Verde

31g CARB PER SERVING

PREP: 20 minutes **SLOW COOK:** 6 to 6½ hours (low) or 3 hours (high)
MAKES: 6 servings (1 cup pork mixture and ½ cup rice each)

1 large onion, cut into thin wedges
1½ pounds boneless pork loin, cut into 1½-inch pieces
2 large tomatoes, coarsely chopped (1⅓ cups)
1 16-ounce jar green salsa (salsa verde)
½ cup reduced-sodium chicken broth
2 cloves garlic, minced
1 teaspoon ground cumin
¼ teaspoon black pepper
3 cups hot cooked brown rice
 Snipped fresh cilantro

1. In a 3½- or 4-quart slow cooker place onion and pork. Top with tomatoes, salsa, broth, garlic, cumin, and pepper.

2. Cover and cook on low-heat setting for 6 to 6½ hours or on high-heat setting for 3 hours. Serve with hot cooked brown rice and top each serving with cilantro.

PER SERVING: 297 cal., 6 g total fat (1 g sat. fat), 78 mg chol., 231 mg sodium, 31 g carb. (3 g fiber, 3 g sugars), 29 g pro. Exchanges: 2 starch, 3 lean meat, 0.5 vegetable.

Cook Well: Should you reach for brown rice or white rice? If you're pressed for time, white is the speedier choice—it's ready in 20 minutes. Brown rice takes longer (about 50 minutes), but the payoff includes a pleasing nutty flavor, a chewy texture, and whole grain goodness.

To cook brown or white rice, pour 2 cups water in a medium saucepan. Bring the water to a full boil; if desired, add ¼ teaspoon salt to the water. Slowly add 1 cup regular brown rice or long grain white rice. Return to boiling; reduce heat. Simmer, covered, about 15 minutes for white rice (45 minutes for regular brown rice) or until most of the water is absorbed and the rice is tender. Let stand, covered, 5 minutes before serving. Makes 3 cups.

Posole Pork Chops

34g CARB PER SERVING

PREP: 25 minutes **SLOW COOK:** 4 to 4½ hours (low) or 2 to 2½ hours (high)
MAKES: 6 servings (3 ounces cooked pork, ⅔ cup vegetable mixture, ¼ cup brown rice, and ¼ cup juices each)

1. Place onion in a 4- to 5-quart slow cooker. Top with pork chops. Top chops with sweet peppers. In a large bowl stir together the tomatoes, hominy, poblano pepper, chili powder, cocoa powder, oregano, and salt. Pour over pork chop mixture in cooker.

2. Cover and cook on low-heat setting for 4 to 4½ hours or on high-heat setting for 2 to 2½ hours.

3. Using a slotted spoon and tongs, transfer meat and vegetables to a serving platter. Serve meat and vegetables over hot cooked rice. Spoon ¼ cup of the juices over each serving and sprinkle with cilantro.

*Test Kitchen Tip: Because chile peppers contain volatile oils that can burn your skin and eyes, avoid direct contact with them as much as possible. When working with chile peppers, wear plastic or rubber gloves. If your bare hands do touch the peppers, wash your hands and nails well with soap and warm water.

PER SERVING: 353 cal., 7 g total fat (2 g sat. fat), 104 mg chol., 419 mg sodium, 34 g carb. (7 g fiber, 6 g sugars), 38 g pro. Exchanges: 2 starch, 4 lean meat, 1 vegetable.

1 medium onion, chopped (½ cup)
6 boneless pork chops, cut ½ to ¾ inch thick (about 2 pounds total)
1 small yellow sweet pepper, cut into strips
1 small red sweet pepper, cut into strips
2 14.5-ounce cans no-salt-added diced tomatoes, undrained
1 15.5-ounce can golden or white hominy, rinsed and drained
¼ cup chopped fresh poblano chile pepper*
1 tablespoon chili powder
1 tablespoon unsweetened cocoa powder
2 teaspoons dried oregano, crushed
¼ teaspoon salt
1½ cups hot cooked brown rice
⅓ cup snipped fresh cilantro

Meatballs with Sweet Lemon Glaze

33g
CARB PER
SERVING

PREP: 25 minutes **SLOW COOK:** 4 hours (low) or 2 hours (high), plus 10 minutes (high)
MAKES: 4 servings (8 meatballs, ¾ cup steamed pea pods, and about 3 tablespoons sauce each)

1. In a large bowl combine green onions, oats, egg, 2 teaspoons of the lemon peel, the crushed red pepper, and salt. Add ground beef; mix well. Form into 1-inch meatballs.
2. Lightly coat an unheated large nonstick skillet with cooking spray; heat over medium-high heat. Brown meatballs in skillet, turning occasionally. Meanwhile, in a small bowl combine spreadable fruit, the water, 1 tablespoon of the soy sauce, and 1 tablespoon of the lemon juice. Lightly coat an unheated 1½- or 2-quart slow cooker with cooking spray. Add meatballs to cooker and pour the fruit spread mixture over all in cooker.
3. Cover and cook on low-heat setting for 4 hours or on high-heat setting for 2 hours.
4. Using a slotted spoon, transfer the meatballs to a plate. In a small bowl whisk together the remaining 1 tablespoon soy sauce, 1 tablespoon lemon juice, the cornstarch, and remaining 1 teaspoon lemon peel. Whisk into the cooking liquid in slow cooker. Gently fold in the meatballs.
5. If using low-heat setting, turn to high-heat setting. Cover and cook about 10 minutes more or until thoroughly heated and sauce is slightly thickened. Serve meatballs over snow peas. If desired, sprinkle with black pepper and serve with lemon wedges.

*Test Kitchen Tip: To steam snow pea pods, place a steamer basket in a saucepan. Add water to just below the bottom of the basket. Bring water to boiling. Add pea pods to steamer basket. Cover and reduce heat. Steam for 2 to 4 minutes or until desired doneness.

PER SERVING: 332 cal., 9 g total fat (3 g sat. fat), 61 mg chol., 511 mg sodium, 33 g carb.
(3 g fiber, 20 g sugars), 29 g pro. Exchanges: 1 starch, 1 fruit, 1 lean meat, 1 vegetable.

- ½ cup finely chopped green onions
- ¼ cup quick-cooking rolled oats
- ¼ cup refrigerated or frozen egg product, thawed
- 3 teaspoons finely shredded lemon peel
- ¼ teaspoon crushed red pepper
- ¼ teaspoon salt
- 1 pound 93 percent lean ground beef, ground pork, or ground turkey
  Nonstick cooking spray
- ½ cup apricot spreadable fruit
- ¼ cup water
- 2 tablespoons reduced-sodium soy sauce
- 2 tablespoons lemon juice
- 2 teaspoons cornstarch
- 4 cups fresh snow pea pods, steamed*
  Freshly ground black pepper (optional)
  Lemon wedges (optional)

Polenta with Ground Beef Ragout

30g
CARB PER
SERVING

PREP: 25 minutes **SLOW COOK:** 7 to 9 hours (low) or 3½ to 4½ hours (high), plus 30 minutes (high)
MAKES: 6 servings (1 cup beef mixture, ⅓ cup polenta, and 2 teaspoons pesto each)

1   **pound extra-lean ground beef**
1   **14.5-ounce can no-salt-added stewed tomatoes, undrained**
3   **medium carrots, cut into ½-inch slices**
2   **medium onions, cut into thin wedges**
½   **cup water**
1   **teaspoon dried Italian seasoning, crushed**
¼   **teaspoon black pepper**
6   **cloves garlic, minced**
1   **large red sweet pepper, cut into 1-inch pieces**
1   **medium zucchini, halved lengthwise and cut into ¼-inch slices**
2   **cups soft cooked polenta**
¼   **cup purchased pesto**
    Fresh basil sprigs (optional)

1. In a large skillet cook ground beef until browned. Drain off fat. Transfer meat to a 3½- or 4-quart slow cooker. Stir in tomatoes, carrots, onions, the water, Italian seasoning, black pepper, and garlic.

2. Cover and cook on low-heat setting for 7 to 9 hours or on high-heat setting for 3½ to 4½ hours.

3. If using low-heat setting, turn to high-heat setting. Stir in sweet pepper and zucchini. Cover and cook about 30 minutes more or until pepper and zucchini are crisp-tender.

4. Serve meat mixture over polenta. Top individual servings with pesto. If desired, garnish with fresh basil.

***Test Kitchen Tip:** Prepare polenta according to the package directions on quick-cooking polenta mix.

PER SERVING: 285 cal., 9 g total fat (3 g sat. fat), 50 mg chol., 488 mg sodium, 30 g carb. (6 g fiber, 9 g sugars), 21 g pro. Exchanges: 1 starch, 2 lean meat, 2 vegetable, 1 fat.

On the Side: Few sides complement a meaty, slow-cooked main dish better than a fresh and bright green salad. Try these combos with a reduced-fat vinaigrette:
- Green-leaf lettuce, green onion slices, orange slices, and reduced-fat feta cheese.
- Romaine lettuce, red onion, chopped cooked beets (available precooked in the produce aisle), reduced-fat blue cheese crumbles, toasted walnuts, and chives.
- Mesclun salad mix, thinly sliced sweet onion, toasted slivered almonds, and dried cherries.
- Arugula, cherry tomatoes, sliced avocado, sliced green onions, and sliced cucumbers.

Mediterranean Meat Loaf

10g CARB PER SERVING

PREP: 25 minutes **SLOW COOK:** 7 to 8 hours (low) or 3½ to 4 hours (high)
MAKES: 6 servings (⅙ of the loaf)

¼ cup refrigerated or frozen egg product, thawed, or 1 egg, lightly beaten
2 tablespoons fat-free milk
½ cup fine dry bread crumbs
½ teaspoon dried oregano, crushed
¼ teaspoon black pepper
2 cloves garlic, minced
1½ pounds 95 percent lean ground beef
½ cup crumbled reduced-fat feta cheese (2 ounces)
¼ cup oil-packed dried tomatoes, drained and snipped
¼ cup bottled pizza or pasta sauce
Romaine leaves, julienne carrots, and cucumber slices (optional)
Red wine vinaigrette (optional)

1. In a large bowl combine egg and milk; beat with a fork. Stir in bread crumbs, oregano, pepper, and garlic. Add ground beef, feta cheese, and dried tomatoes; mix well. Shape meat mixture into a 6-inch round loaf.

2. Tear off an 18×18-inch sheet of heavy foil into thirds. Fold each piece into thirds lengthwise. Crisscross strips and place meat loaf in center of foil strips. Bring up strips and transfer loaf and foil to a 3½- or 4-quart slow cooker (leave foil strips under loaf). Press loaf away from side of cooker. Fold strips down, leaving loaf exposed. Spread pizza sauce over loaf.

3. Cover and cook on low-heat setting for 7 to 8 hours or on high-heat setting for 3½ to 4 hours.

4. Using foil strips, carefully lift meat loaf from cooker. Discard foil strips. If desired, combine romaine, carrots, and cucumbers; top with vinaigrette. Serve salad with meat loaf.

PER SERVING: 238 cal., 9 g total fat (4 g sat. fat), 74 mg chol., 324 mg sodium, 10 g carb. (1 g fiber, 1 g sugars), 29 g pro. Exchanges: 0.5 starch, 4 lean meat, 1 fat.

On the Side: Few sides go better with meat loaf than potatoes. Ready-made potato products can be high in fat and calories. Keep your meal plan in line with homemade roasted potatoes.

To roast potatoes: Scrub 3 medium round red potatoes (1 pound) and cut each into eighths. Place in a 9×9×2-inch baking pan. Sprinkle lightly with salt and black pepper and drizzle with a small amount of olive oil, tossing to coat. Roast, uncovered, in a 425°F oven for 25 to 30 minutes or until potatoes are tender and browned on the edges, stirring occasionally.

Beef Burgundy

27 g CARB PER SERVING

PREP: 45 minutes **SLOW COOK:** 8 to 10 hours (low) or 4 to 5 hours (high)
MAKES: 8 servings (¾ cup meat mixture and about ½ cup potatoes each)

2 pounds boneless beef chuck pot roast, cut into 1-inch pieces
2 teaspoons olive oil
3 medium onions, chopped (1½ cups)
4 medium carrots, cut into ¾-inch pieces
2 cups frozen small whole onions
2 cloves garlic, minced
2 tablespoons quick-cooking tapioca, crushed
1 cup Burgundy wine or lower-sodium beef broth
½ cup lower-sodium beef broth
¼ cup brandy or lower-sodium beef broth
1 tablespoon tomato paste
1 teaspoon dried thyme, crushed
½ teaspoon dried rosemary, crushed
½ teaspoon black pepper
2 bay leaves
1 cup quartered fresh cremini mushrooms
2 teaspoons olive oil
1 recipe Skins-On Garlic Mashed Potatoes
  Snipped fresh thyme or Italian (flat-leaf) parsley

1. In a large nonstick skillet brown half of the beef in 1 teaspoon of the oil over medium-high heat; remove from skillet. Repeat with remaining beef and 1 teaspoon oil.
2. In a 3½- or 4-quart slow cooker place chopped onions, carrots, whole onions, and garlic. Sprinkle with tapioca. Place beef on top of vegetables in cooker. In a medium bowl whisk together wine, broth, brandy, tomato paste, dried thyme, rosemary, and pepper. Pour over all in cooker. Add bay leaves, tucking them down into the liquid.
3. Cover and cook on low-heat setting for 8 to 10 hours or on high-heat setting for 4 to 5 hours. Discard the bay leaves.
4. Near the end of cooking time, in a large skillet cook mushrooms in 2 teaspoons hot oil over medium-high heat until browned. Serve beef mixture with Skins-On Garlic Mashed Potatoes. Top each serving with mushroom and fresh thyme.

Skins-On Garlic Mashed Potatoes: Cut 1⅓ pounds red-skin, Yukon gold, or russet potatoes into quarters. In a covered large saucepan cook potatoes and 4 cloves garlic, peeled and halved, in enough boiling lightly salted water to cover for 20 to 25 minutes or until tender; drain. Mash with potato masher or beat with an electric mixer on low speed. Add 1 tablespoon butter, ⅛ teaspoon salt, and ⅛ teaspoon black pepper. Slowly beat in 3 to 5 tablespoons fat-free milk until potato mixture is light and fluffy.

PER SERVING: 323 cal., 9 g total fat (3 g sat. fat), 65 mg chol., 229 mg sodium, 27 g carb. (4 g fiber, 6 g sugars), 24 g pro. Exchanges: 1.5 starch, 3 lean meat, 1 vegetable, 1 fat.

Pot Roast and Onions

5 g CARB PER SERVING

PREP: 15 minutes **SLOW COOK:** 8 to 10 hours (low) or 4 to 5 hours (high)
MAKES: 8 servings (3 ounces meat and about 3 tablespoons sauce each)

1. Trim fat from roast. If necessary, cut roast to fit in a 3½- or 4-quart slow cooker. Place roast in the cooker. Top with onions. In a small bowl combine tomato sauce, the ¼ cup water, the mustard, horseradish, salt, and pepper; pour over all in cooker.
2. Cover and cook on low-heat setting for 8 to 10 hours or on high-heat setting for 4 to 5 hours.
3. Transfer meat and onions to a serving platter; cover to keep warm. For sauce, transfer cooking liquid to a small saucepan; skim off fat. In a small bowl stir together flour and the 2 tablespoons cold water. Stir into mixture in saucepan. Cook and stir over medium heat until thickened and bubbly; cook and stir for 1 minute more. Serve the sauce with roast and onions. If desired, served with steamed broccoli.

PER SERVING: 170 cal., 5 g total fat (2 g sat. fat), 67 mg chol., 376 mg sodium, 5 g carb. (1 g fiber, 1 g sugars), 25 g pro. Exchanges: 3.5 lean meat, 0.5 vegetable, 1 fat.

1 **2- to 2½-pound boneless beef chuck pot roast**
2 **medium onions, cut into wedges**
1 **8-ounce can tomato sauce**
¼ **cup water**
1 **tablespoon yellow mustard**
1 **to 2 teaspoons prepared horseradish**
½ **teaspoon salt**
¼ **teaspoon black pepper**
2 **tablespoons flour**
2 **tablespoons cold water**
Steamed broccoli (optional)

Steak with Tuscan Tomato Sauce

PREP: 25 minutes **SLOW COOK:** 8 to 10 hours (low) or 4 to 5 hours (high)
MAKES: 4 servings (3 ounces meat and about ⅓ cup sauce per serving each)

1 **pound boneless beef round steak, cut 1 inch thick**
1 **tablespoon vegetable oil**
1 **medium onion, sliced (½ cup)**
2 **tablespoons quick-cooking tapioca, crushed**
1 **teaspoon dried thyme, crushed**
¼ **teaspoon black pepper**
1 **14.5-ounce can diced tomatoes with basil, garlic, and oregano, undrained**
2 **cups hot cooked red chard, noodles, or brown rice (optional)**

1. Trim fat from steak. In a large skillet brown steak on all sides in hot oil over medium heat. Drain off fat.

2. Place onion in a 3½- or 4-quart slow cooker. Sprinkle with tapioca, thyme, and pepper. Pour tomatoes over onion in cooker. Place steak on mixture in cooker.

3. Cover and cook on low-heat setting for 8 to 10 hours or on high-heat setting for 4 to 5 hours.

4. Transfer meat to a cutting board. Slice meat; serve with cooking sauce and, if desired, hot cooked chard, noodles, or rice.

PER SERVING: 230 cal., 6 g total fat (1 g sat. fat), 49 mg chol., 595 mg sodium, 16 g carb. (1 g fiber, 7 g sugars), 28 g pro. Exchanges: 0.5 starch, 2.5 lean meat, 1 vegetable.

Lamb and Lentil Shepherd's Pie

43g
CARB PER SERVING

PREP: 20 minutes **SLOW COOK:** 6 to 8 hours (low) or 3 to 4 hours (high)
MAKES: 8 servings (1 cup meat mixture and ⅓ cup potatoes each)

1 pound lean ground lamb or beef
1 large onion, chopped (1 cup)
1 16-ounce package frozen mixed vegetables
1 14.5-ounce can lower-sodium beef broth
1 14.5-ounce can no-salt-added diced tomatoes with basil, garlic, and oregano, undrained
1 10.75-ounce can reduced-fat and reduced-sodium condensed tomato soup
1 cup dry brown lentils, rinsed and drained
¼ teaspoon crushed red pepper
2⅔ cups prepared mashed potatoes

1. In a large skillet cook ground lamb and onion until meat is browned and onion is tender; drain off fat.
2. In a 3½- or 4-quart slow cooker combine meat mixture, frozen vegetables, broth, tomatoes, tomato soup, lentils, and crushed red pepper.
3. Cover and cook on low-heat setting for 6 to 8 hours or on high-heat setting for 3 to 4 hours. Serve meat and lentil mixture over potatoes.

PER SERVING: 317 cal., 6 g total fat (2 g sat. fat), 36 mg chol., 429 mg sodium, 43 g carb. (14 g fiber, 8 g sugars), 24 g pro. Exchanges: 2.5 carb., 2 lean meat, 0.5 vegetable.

Time-Saving Trick: Fresh-made mashed potatoes add a homey touch. But if you are short on time, pick up a bag of refrigerated mashed potatoes to serve with this humble stewlike mixture.

Spicy Lamb Shanks

17g
CARB PER
SERVING

PREP: 25 minutes **SLOW COOK:** 11 to 12 hours (low) or 5½ to 6 hours (high)
MAKES: 6 servings (9 ounces meat with bone, ½ cup vegetables, and ¼ cup sauce each)

2 **large oranges**
5 **medium carrots, cut into 2-inch pieces**
1½ **cups frozen small whole onions**
4 **large cloves garlic, thinly sliced**
4 **meaty lamb shanks (about 4 pounds total)**
6 **inches stick cinnamon, broken into 1-inch pieces**
1¼ **cups lower-sodium beef broth**
1½ **teaspoons ground cardamom**
1 **teaspoon ground cumin**
½ **teaspoon ground turmeric**
½ **teaspoon black pepper**
2 **tablespoons cold water**
4 **teaspoons cornstarch**
⅓ **cup pitted Kalamata or other ripe olives, halved**
1 **tablespoon snipped fresh cilantro (optional)**

1. Using a vegetable peeler, remove the peel from one of the oranges, avoiding the bitter white pith. Cut peel into thin strips to make about ¼ cup. Squeeze juice from both oranges to make about ⅔ cup; set aside.
2. In a 5- to 6-quart slow cooker combine carrots, onions, and garlic. Add orange peel strips, lamb shanks, and stick cinnamon. In a small bowl stir together orange juice, beef broth, cardamom, cumin, turmeric, and pepper; pour over all in cooker.
3. Cover and cook on low-heat setting for 11 to 12 hours or on high-heat setting for 5½ to 6 hours. Discard stick cinnamon pieces.
4. Using a slotted spoon, transfer meat and vegetables to a serving platter; cover to keep warm.
5. For sauce, pour cooking liquid into a glass measuring cup; skim off fat. Measure 1½ cups of the cooking liquid. In a small saucepan stir together the cold water and cornstarch until smooth. Stir in the 1½ cups cooking liquid. Cook and stir over medium heat until thickened and bubbly; cook and stir for 2 minutes more. Serve sauce with meat and vegetables. Sprinkle with olives and, if desired, cilantro.

PER SERVING: 223 cal., 5 g total fat (1 g sat. fat), 85 mg chol., 313 mg sodium, 17 g carb. (4 g fiber, 8 g sugars), 28 g pro. Exchanges: 0.5 carb., 3.5 lean meat, 1 vegetable.

Cheesy Noodle Casserole

31g CARB PER SERVING

PREP: 25 minutes **SLOW COOK:** 7 to 8 hours (low) or 3½ to 4 hours (high), plus 20 to 30 minutes (high)
MAKES: 8 servings (1 cup each)

1. In a 3½- or 4-quart slow cooker whisk together the water and cream of mushroom soup. Stir in tomatoes, celery, carrots, onion, Italian seasoning, garlic, salt, and pepper.
2. Cover and cook on low-heat setting for 7 to 8 hours or high-heat setting for 3½ to 4 hours.
3. If using low-heat setting, turn to high-heat setting. Stir in uncooked noodles; cover and cook for 20 to 30 minutes more or until noodles are tender, stirring once halfway through cooking. Gently stir in tofu cubes. Sprinkle with cheese; cover and let stand until cheese is melted.

*Test Kitchen Tip: To drain tofu, place it on a paper towel-lined plate for 15 minutes.

PER SERVING: 245 cal., 7 g total fat (2 g sat. fat), 33 mg chol., 319 mg sodium, 31 g carb. (4 g fiber, 4 g sugars), 13 g pro. Exchanges: 2 starch, 1 medium-fat meat, 1 vegetable.

2½ cups water
1 10.75-ounce can reduced-fat and reduced-sodium condensed cream of mushroom soup
1 14.5-ounce can no-salt-added diced tomatoes, undrained
2 stalks celery, sliced (1 cup)
2 medium carrots, sliced (1 cup)
1 large onion, chopped (1 cup)
1½ teaspoons dried Italian seasoning, crushed
2 cloves garlic, minced
¼ teaspoon salt
¼ teaspoon black pepper
8 ounces dried extra-wide noodles (about 4 cups dried)
1 16-ounce package extra-firm tofu (fresh bean curd), drained if necessary and cubed*
½ cup shredded reduced-fat cheddar cheese (2 ounces)

Black Beans and Avocado on Quinoa

39g CARB PER SERVING

PREP: 20 minutes **STAND:** 1 hour 15 minutes **SLOW COOK:** 10 hours (low) or 5 hours (high)
MAKES: 6 servings (½ cup spinach, ⅓ cup quinoa, ⅔ cup bean mixture, and ¼ cup avocado each)

6 **ounces dried black beans (¾ cup)**
5 **cups water**
   Nonstick cooking spray
1 **large onion, chopped (1 cup)**
10 **ounces grape tomatoes, halved**
1 **teaspoon ground cumin**
½ **cup chopped fresh cilantro**
2 **tablespoons lime juice**
1 **tablespoon olive oil**
½ **teaspoon salt**
2 **cups cooked quinoa**
¼ **cup chopped fresh cilantro**
1 **tablespoon olive oil**
¼ **teaspoon salt**
3 **cups fresh arugula or spinach**
1 **ripe medium avocado, peeled, seeded, and chopped**
1 **medium lime, cut into six wedges**

1. Rinse beans; drain. In a large saucepan combine beans and 3 cups of the water. Bring to boiling; reduce heat. Simmer, uncovered, for 10 minutes. Remove from heat. Cover and let stand for 1 hour. Drain and rinse beans.

2. Lightly coat an unheated 3- or 3½-quart slow cooker with cooking spray. Place beans in cooker. Stir in the remaining 2 cups water, the onion, half of the tomatoes, and the cumin.

3. Cover and cook on low-heat setting for 10 hours or on high-heat setting for 5 hours or until beans are soft. Stir in the remaining tomatoes, the ½ cup cilantro, the lime juice, 1 tablespoon oil, and the ½ teaspoon salt. Let stand at least 15 minutes to develop flavors.

4. Before serving, toss the quinoa with the ¼ cup cilantro, 1 tablespoon oil, and the ¼ teaspoon salt. Divide arugula among six serving plates. Spoon the quinoa mixture over the arugula. Spoon bean mixture over the quinoa. Top with avocado and serve with lime wedges.

PER SERVING: 277 cal., 10 g total fat (1 g sat. fat), 0 mg chol., 321 mg sodium, 39 g carb. (9 g fiber, 3 g sugars), 11 g pro. Exchanges: 2 starch, 1 lean meat, 1 vegetable, 1 fat.

ready when you are

Here's slow cooking at its fix-and-forget best! Most of these recipes require 10 or more hours of low-and-slow simmering, making them perfect to prep in the morning and savor at the end of a long day.

Chicken Ragout

33g CARB PER SERVING

PREP: 20 minutes **SLOW COOK:** 8 to 10 hours (low) **COOK:** 8 minutes
MAKES: 8 servings (1 cup chicken mixture and about ⅓ cup noodles each)

8 **chicken thighs (about 3½ pounds total), skinned**
2 **14.5-ounce cans no-salt-added diced tomatoes, drained**
3 **cups 1-inch carrot slices or baby carrots**
1 **large onion, cut into wedges (1 cup)**
⅓ **cup reduced-sodium chicken broth**
2 **tablespoons white wine vinegar**
1 **teaspoon dried rosemary, crushed**
1 **teaspoon dried thyme, crushed**
¼ **teaspoon black pepper**
8 **ounces fresh button mushrooms, sliced**
1 **teaspoon olive oil**
3 **cups hot cooked whole wheat noodles**
   Snipped fresh parsley (optional)

1. Place chicken thighs in a 3½- or 4-quart slow cooker. In a large bowl stir together tomatoes, carrots, onion, broth, vinegar, rosemary, thyme, and pepper. Pour over chicken in cooker.
2. Cover and cook on low-heat setting for 8 to 10 hours.
3. Just before serving, in a large nonstick skillet cook and stir mushrooms in hot oil over medium-high heat for 8 to 10 minutes or until golden. Remove chicken from cooker. Remove chicken from bones; discard bones. Stir chicken and mushrooms into mixture in cooker. Serve chicken mixture over hot cooked noodles. If desired, sprinkle each serving with parsley.

PER SERVING: 234 cal., 4 g total fat (1 g sat. fat), 57 mg chol., 163 mg sodium, 33 g carb. (7 g fiber, 7 g sugars), 20 g pro. Exchanges: 1.5 starch, 2 lean meat, 1.5 vegetable.

Cook Well: To make sure you're getting whole grain nutrients in pasta, take a look at the ingredient listing. If the first ingredient listed contains the word "whole," that's a good sign (though not a guarantee) that the product is predominantly whole grain.

Also look for the Whole Grain Stamp. This official packaging stamp from the Whole Grains Council helps consumers identify foods that contain significant amounts of whole grains. The 100% Stamp indicates that all the grain in the product is whole grain; the Basic Stamp indicates that each serving contains at least 8 grams of whole grain.

Potato, Sausage, and Egg Breakfast

23g CARB PER SERVING

PREP: 15 minutes **SLOW COOK:** 10 hours (low) **COOK:** 3 minutes
MAKES: 6 servings (1 cup sausage-vegetable mixture, 1 egg, and about 1 tablespoon cheese each)

Nonstick cooking spray
1½ pounds red or yellow potatoes, cut into 1½-inch pieces
12 ounces uncooked chicken sausage links, cut into 1-inch slices
1 large onion, cut into wedges
1 small red sweet pepper, cut into 1-inch strips
1 small green sweet pepper, cut into 1-inch strips
¼ cup reduced-sodium chicken broth
½ teaspoon dried thyme, crushed
¼ teaspoon black pepper
6 eggs
Black pepper
½ cup shredded reduced-fat cheddar cheese (2 ounces)

1. Coat a 20×18-inch sheet of heavy foil with cooking spray. Place potatoes, sausage, onion, and sweet peppers on foil. Drizzle with broth. Sprinkle with thyme and the ¼ teaspoon black pepper. Bring up long sides of foil and fold to seal. Roll up short sides of foil to enclose. If necessary, manipulate foil packet to fit in an oval 3½- or 4-quart slow cooker. Place packet in cooker.
2. Cover and cook on low-heat setting for 10 hours.
3. To poach eggs, half-fill a very large skillet with water and bring to boiling; reduce heat to simmering (bubbles should begin to break the surface of the water). Break an egg into a cup and slip egg into the simmering water. Repeat with remaining eggs, allowing each egg an equal amount of space in the water. Simmer eggs, uncovered, for 3 to 5 minutes or until whites are set and yolks begin to thicken but are not hard. Remove eggs with a slotted spoon.
4. Carefully open the foil packet to avoid getting burned by escaping steam. To serve, spoon sausage and vegetables onto serving plates. Place a poached egg on top of each serving and sprinkle egg with additional black pepper. Sprinkle cheese on individual servings.

PER SERVING: 281 cal., 12 g total fat (4 g sat. fat), 262 mg chol., 485 mg sodium, 23 g carb. (3 g fiber, 3 g sugars), 21 g pro. Exchanges: 1 starch, 2.5 medium-fat meat, 1 vegetable.

Chicken Vera Cruz

25g
CARB PER
SERVING

PREP: 25 minutes **SLOW COOK:** 10 hours (low)
MAKES: 6 servings (1 chicken thigh, ¾ cup vegetable mixture, and about 2 tablespoons topping each)

1 **medium onion, cut into wedges**

1 **pound yellow-skin potatoes, cut into 1-inch pieces**

6 **skinless, boneless chicken thighs (about 1¼ pounds total)**

2 **14.5-ounce cans no-salt-added diced tomatoes, undrained**

1 **fresh jalapeño chile pepper, seeded and sliced***

2 **tablespoons Worcestershire sauce**

1 **tablespoon chopped garlic**

1 **teaspoon dried oregano, crushed**

¼ **teaspoon ground cinnamon**

⅛ **teaspoon ground cloves**

1 **recipe Parsley-Olive Topping**

1. Place onion in a 3½- or 4-quart slow cooker. Top with potatoes and chicken thighs. Drain juices from one can of tomatoes and discard the juice. In a bowl stir together the drained and undrained tomatoes, the jalapeño pepper, Worcestershire sauce, garlic, oregano, cinnamon, and cloves. Pour over all in cooker.

2. Cover and cook on low-heat setting for 10 hours. Sprinkle Parsley-Olive Topping over individual servings.

Parsley-Olive Topping: In a small bowl stir together ½ cup snipped fresh parsley and ¼ cup chopped pimiento-stuffed green olives.

***Test Kitchen Tip:** Because chile peppers contain volatile oils that can burn your skin and eyes, avoid direct contact with them as much as possible. When working with chile peppers, wear plastic or rubber gloves. If your bare hands do touch the peppers, wash your hands and nails well with soap and warm water.

PER SERVING: 228 cal., 5 g total fat (1 g sat. fat), 78 mg chol., 287 mg sodium, 25 g carb., (5 g fiber, 9 g sugars), 22 g pro. Exchanges: 1.5 starch, 2.5 lean meat, 1 vegetable.

Seeded Fennel Pork Shoulder

17g CARB PER SERVING

PREP: 30 minutes **SLOW COOK:** 10 to 12 hours (low)
MAKES: 6 servings (4 ounces cooked meat and ¼ cup fennel mixture each)

1. Place quartered fennel, halved apple, onion, and raisins in a 4- to 5-quart slow cooker.
2. Trim fat from roast. Spread mustard all over roast. In a small bowl combine fennel seeds, celery seeds, dill seeds, mustard seeds, and cracked black pepper. Sprinkle seed mixture evenly over roast to coat. Place coated roast on top of fennel mixture in cooker. Pour apple cider over all in cooker.
3. Cover and cook on low-heat setting for 10 to 12 hours.
4. Remove roast from cooker; cover and keep warm. Discard liquid and solids in cooker. In a small saucepan bring apple jelly to boiling. Remove from heat and stir in slivered fennel and sliced apple until coated. Spoon apple mixture over roast before serving.

PER SERVING: 280 cal., 9 g total fat (3 g sat. fat), 93 mg chol., 238 mg sodium, 17 g carb. (2 g fiber, 12 g sugars), 30 g pro. Exchanges: 1 carb., 4 lean meat, 0.5 fat.

1 large fennel bulb, trimmed and quartered
1 large tart apple, cored and halved
1 small onion, halved
¼ cup golden raisins
1 3-pound boneless pork shoulder roast
2 tablespoons Dijon-style mustard
1 teaspoon fennel seeds, crushed
1 teaspoon celery seeds, crushed
1 teaspoon dill seeds, crushed
1 teaspoon mustard seeds
½ teaspoon cracked black pepper
⅔ cup apple cider or apple juice
½ cup low-sugar apple jelly
1 small fennel bulb, trimmed and cut into thin slivers
1 small tart apple, cut into very thin slices

Pork Roast and Harvest Vegetables

32g CARB PER SERVING

PREP: 30 minutes **SLOW COOK:** 10 to 12 hours (low) or 5 to 6 hours (high)
MAKES: 6 servings (3 ounces cooked pork, ¾ cup vegetables, and ¼ cup liquid each)

1. Trim fat from roast. If necessary, cut roast to fit into a 3½- to 5-quart slow cooker. In a large skillet heat oil over medium heat. Add roast; cook until browned, turning to brown evenly on all sides. In cooker combine parsnips, carrots, sweet pepper, and celery. Sprinkle vegetables with tapioca.
2. In a small bowl combine apple juice concentrate, the water, bouillon granules, ¼ teaspoon cinnamon, and the black pepper. Pour over vegetables. Place roast on top of vegetables.
3. Cover and cook on low-heat setting for 10 to 12 hours or on high-heat setting for 5 to 6 hours.
4. Transfer meat and vegetables to a serving platter. Strain cooking liquid; skim off fat. Drizzle some of the cooking liquid over meat; pass remaining cooking liquid. If desired, sprinkle with ⅛ teaspoon cinnamon.

PER SERVING: 309 cal., 9 g total fat (3 g sat. fat), 73 mg chol., 272 mg sodium, 32 g carb., (4 g fiber, 3 g sugars), 24 g pro. Exchanges: 2 carb., 3 lean meat, 1 vegetable.

1 1½- to 2-pound boneless pork shoulder roast
1 tablespoon vegetable oil
3 medium parsnips, cut into ½-inch pieces (2 cups)
3 medium carrots, cut into ½-inch pieces (1½ cups)
1 large green sweet pepper, cut into bite-size pieces
2 stalks celery, cut into ½-inch pieces (1 cup)
3 tablespoons quick-cooking tapioca, crushed
1 6-ounce can frozen apple juice concentrate, thawed
¼ cup water
1 teaspoon instant beef bouillon granules
¼ teaspoon ground cinnamon
¼ teaspoon black pepper
⅛ teaspoon ground cinnamon (optional)

Shredded Pork with Fruit Relish

5 g
CARB PER SERVING

PREP: 25 minutes **SLOW COOK:** 10 to 12 hours (low)
MAKES: 10 servings (3 ounces cooked meat and about 3 tablespoons relish each)

3 to 4 cooking apples, cored and halved
1 3½-pound boneless pork shoulder roast
¼ teaspoon salt
¼ teaspoon black pepper
½ cup mango nectar
1 recipe Fruit Relish
Lime wedges

1. Place apples in a 4- to 5-quart slow cooker. Trim fat from roast; season roast with the salt and black pepper. Place roast on top of apples. Pour mango nectar over roast in cooker.
2. Cover and cook on low-heat setting for 10 to 12 hours.
3. Remove roast from cooker; discard apples and cooking liquid. Using two forks, shred meat. Serve meat with Fruit Relish and lime wedges.

Fruit Relish: In a small bowl combine 1 cup finely chopped fresh pineapple, 1 cup finely chopped papaya, ¾ cup finely chopped red sweet pepper, 1 tablespoon lime juice, and 1 teaspoon canola oil. Cover and chill for up to 12 hours.

PER SERVING: 245 cal., 10 g total fat (3 g sat. fat), 103 mg chol., 190 mg sodium, 5 g carb. (1 g fiber, 3 g sugars), 32 g pro. Exchanges: 4.5 lean meat, 1 fat.

On the Side: A side of sweet potatoes complements this dish and boosts your intake of vitamins and A and C. Try sweet potatoes baked, roasted, or even mashed.

Southwestern Sweet Potato Stew

42g CARB PER SERVING

PREP: 15 minutes **SLOW COOK:** 10 to 12 hours (low)
MAKES: 6 servings (1⅓ cups each)

1. In a 3½- or 4-quart slow cooker combine vegetable broth, the water, sweet potatoes, onion, garlic, oregano, chili powder, cumin, and salt. Stir in hominy, beans, and poblano pepper.
2. Cover and cook on low-heat setting for 10 to 12 hours.
3. Use a potato masher to coarsely mash the sweet potatoes. Sprinkle individual servings with snipped cilantro. Serve with lime wedges.

*Test Kitchen Tip: To roast a poblano chile pepper, preheat oven to 425°F. Cut pepper in half lengthwise; remove stem, seeds, and membranes. Place pepper halves, cut sides down, on a foil-lined baking sheet. Roast for 15 to 20 minutes or until pepper is charred and very tender. Bring foil up around pepper and fold edges together to enclose. Let stand about 15 minutes or until cool enough to handle. Use a sharp knife to loosen edges of the skin; gently pull off the skin in strips and discard.

**Test Kitchen Tip: Because chile peppers contain volatile oils that can burn your skin and eyes, avoid direct contact with them as much as possible. When working with chile peppers, wear plastic or rubber gloves. If your bare hands do touch the peppers, wash your hands and nails well with soap and warm water.

PER SERVING: 202 cal., 1 g total fat (0 g sat. fat), 0 mg chol., 491 mg sodium, 42 g carb. (8 g fiber, 5 g sugars), 7 g pro. Exchanges: 2 starch, 2 vegetable.

2 cups lower-sodium vegetable broth
2 cups water
1½ pounds sweet potatoes, peeled and cut into 2-inch pieces
1 medium onion, chopped (½ cup)
2 cloves garlic, minced
1½ teaspoons dried oregano, crushed
1 teaspoon chili powder
½ teaspoon ground cumin
¼ teaspoon salt
1 15-ounce can golden hominy, rinsed and drained
1 15-ounce can no-salt-added black beans, rinsed and drained
1 fresh poblano chile pepper, roasted,* and cut into thin strips**
Snipped fresh cilantro
Lime wedges

Lentil Taco Salad

40g CARB PER SERVING

PREP: 20 minutes **SLOW COOK:** 10 to 12 hours (low), plus 20 minutes (high)
MAKES: 8 servings (¾ cup lentil mixture, ¾ cup lettuce, ¼ cup tomato, 1 tablespoon cheese, 1½ tablespoons yogurt, and about ¼ cup chips each)

2 large red and/or green sweet peppers, coarsely chopped (2 cups)
1 large onion, chopped (1 cup)
1 cup dry brown lentils, rinsed and drained
½ cup uncooked regular brown rice
3 cloves garlic, minced
2 teaspoons chili powder
¼ teaspoon salt
2 14.5-ounce cans reduced-sodium chicken or vegetable broth
1 medium yellow summer squash, quartered lengthwise and sliced ½ inch thick (1½ cups)
6 cups mixed salad greens
2 cups chopped tomatoes
½ cup shredded reduced-fat cheddar cheese (2 ounces)
¾ cup plain nonfat Greek yogurt
3 ounces multigrain tortilla chips, broken (about 2 cups)

1. In a 3½- or 4-quart slow cooker combine sweet peppers, onion, lentils, rice, garlic, chili powder, and salt. Pour broth over all in cooker.
2. Cover and cook on low-heat setting for 10 to 12 hours. Turn to high-heat setting. Stir in squash. Cover and cook for 20 minutes more.
3. To serve, arrange salad greens on eight dinner plates. Spoon lentil mixture over greens. Top with tomatoes and sprinkle with cheese. Add a spoonful of yogurt to each serving. Sprinkle with tortilla chips.

PER SERVING: 262 cal., 6 g total fat (1 g sat. fat), 5 mg chol., 446 mg sodium, 40 g carb. (11 g fiber, 7 g sugars), 15 g pro. Exchanges: 2 starch, 1 lean meat, 1 vegetable, 0.5 fat.

Layered Brisket Dinner

PREP: 20 minutes **SLOW COOK:** 10 to 12 hours (low)
MAKES: 8 servings (2/3 cup meat, about 1/2 cup vegetables, and 1 tablespoon sauce each)

1 **3-pound fresh beef brisket**
1 **tablespoon Dijon-style mustard**
1 **tablespoon Worcestershire sauce**
1 **tablespoon balsamic vinegar**
1/4 **teaspoon black pepper**
1 **pound baby red or yellow potatoes, halved if large**
1 **8-ounce package baby carrots (2 cups)**
1 **small onion, cut into wedges**
2 **teaspoons olive oil**
1/2 **teaspoon dried Italian seasoning, crushed**
1/4 **teaspoon salt**
1/4 **teaspoon black pepper**
1 **recipe Tangy Mustard Sauce**

1. Trim fat from brisket. Place brisket in a 5- to 6-quart slow cooker. In a small bowl stir together the mustard, Worcestershire sauce, vinegar, and 1/4 teaspoon pepper. Pour over brisket, turning brisket to coat both sides.
2. On a 20×18-inch sheet of heavy foil place the potatoes, carrots, and onion. Drizzle with olive oil and sprinkle with Italian seasoning, salt, and 1/4 teaspoon pepper. Bring up long sides of foil and fold to seal. Roll up short sides of foil to enclose vegetables. If necessary, manipulate foil packet to fit in cooker, making sure the brisket is completely covered with the foil packet.
3. Cover and cook on low-heat setting for 10 to 12 hours.
4. Remove foil packet and brisket from cooker. Slice the brisket across the grain or shred the meat using two forks. Carefully open the foil packet to avoid getting burned by escaping steam. Serve meat and vegetables with Tangy Mustard Sauce.

Tangy Mustard Sauce: In a small bowl combine 1/2 cup light sour cream; 1 1/2 teaspoons Dijon-style mustard; 1/2 teaspoon dried Italian seasoning, crushed; and, if desired, 1/2 teaspoon snipped fresh thyme. Chill sauce in refrigerator. If desired, sprinkle with additional snipped fresh thyme before serving.

PER SERVING: 273 cal., 11 g total fat (4 g sat. fat), 78 mg chol., 289 mg sodium, 14 g carb. (2 g fiber, 3 g sugars), 27 g pro. Exchanges: 1 starch, 3.5 lean meat, 1 fat.

Mediterranean Chuck Roast

8 g
CARB PER SERVING

PREP: 15 minutes **SLOW COOK:** 10 hours (low)
MAKES: 6 servings (3 ounces cooked meat and about 1 tablespoon persillade each)

1. Trim fat from roast. Place garlic cloves and dried tomatoes in a 3½- or 4-quart slow cooker. Top with roast. Pour broth over all in cooker. Sprinkle roast with vinegar, Italian seasoning, and pepper.
2. Cover and cook on low-heat setting for 10 hours. Remove roast from cooker. Using two forks, shred roast or slice the meat. Sprinkle with Olive Persillade. If desired, garnish with lemon wedges.

Olive Persillade: In a small bowl stir together ¼ cup snipped fresh parsley, 1 to 2 tablespoons chopped pitted Kalamata olives, and 1 teaspoon finely shredded lemon peel.

PER SERVING: 240 cal., 7 g total fat (2 g sat. fat), 67 mg chol., 262 mg sodium, 8 g carb. (1 g fiber, 2 g sugars), 35 g pro. Exchanges: 4 lean meat, 1 vegetable, 1 fat.

1 **2-pound beef chuck pot roast**
30 **cloves garlic, peeled**
¼ **cup snipped dried tomatoes (not oil-packed)**
½ **cup beef broth**
2 **tablespoons balsamic vinegar**
1 **teaspoon dried Italian seasoning, crushed**
¼ **teaspoon black pepper**
1 **recipe Olive Persillade Lemon wedges (optional)**

Cook Well: Classic persillade, a combination of fresh garlic and fresh parsley, adds a bright jolt of freshness to slow-cooked dishes.

To make enough of the topper for four servings, mince 2 garlic cloves and ¼ cup fresh parsley together. Sprinkle over stews, roasts, and other meaty dishes just before you serve them.

Lamb and Rice

21g CARB PER SERVING

PREP: 15 minutes **SLOW COOK:** 10 to 12 hours (low)
MAKES: 6 servings (⅔ cup lamb mixture and ⅓ cup rice each)

2 **pounds boneless lamb shoulder**
1 **14.5-ounce can diced tomatoes, undrained**
1 **medium onion, chopped (½ cup)**
6 **cloves garlic, minced**
1 **fresh serrano chile pepper, seeded and chopped***
1 **teaspoon ground ginger**
1 **teaspoon ground coriander**
½ **teaspoon dry mustard**
¼ **teaspoon salt**
⅛ **teaspoon cayenne pepper (optional)**
2 **cups hot cooked brown rice**
   Sliced fresh serrano chile pepper* (optional)

1. Trim fat from lamb and cut meat into 2-inch cubes. Place lamb in a 3½- or 4-quart slow cooker. In a medium bowl stir together tomatoes, onion, garlic, the chopped chile pepper, ginger, coriander, mustard, salt, and cayenne pepper (if desired). Pour mixture over lamb in cooker. Stir to combine.

2. Cover and cook on low-heat setting for 10 to 12 hours. Using a slotted spoon, remove lamb from cooker and serve over hot cooked rice. Skim fat from cooking liquid in cooker and discard fat. Drizzle some of the liquid over lamb and rice just before serving. If desired, garnish with chile pepper slices.

***Test Kitchen Tip:** Because chile peppers contain volatile oils that can burn your skin and eyes, avoid direct contact with them as much as possible. When working with chile peppers, wear plastic or rubber gloves. If your bare hands do touch the peppers, wash your hands and nails well with soap and warm water. For more heat, include the chile pepper seeds.

PER SERVING: 330 cal., 12 g total fat (4 g sat. fat), 101 mg chol., 321 mg sodium, 21 g carb. (2 g fiber, 3 g sugars), 32 g pro. Exchanges: 1 starch, 4 lean meat, 1 vegetable, 1 fat.

cook once, eat thrice

Who knew your slow cooker was as good at multitasking as you are? The four master recipes in this chapter each offer three completely different (and thoroughly delicious) ways to bring great food to the table.

Shredded Chicken

PREP: 20 minutes **SLOW COOK:** 7 to 8 hours (low) or 3½ to 4 hours (high)
MAKES: 12 servings (½ cup each)

4½ **to 5 pounds chicken thighs, skinned**
 4 **fresh thyme sprigs**
 4 **fresh parsley stems**
 2 **bay leaves**
 2 **cloves garlic, halved**
 ½ **teaspoon whole black peppercorns**
 1 **32-ounce box reduced-sodium chicken broth**

1. Place chicken thighs in a 4- to 5-quart slow cooker. For the bouquet garni, place thyme sprigs, parsley stems, bay leaves, garlic, and peppercorns in the center of a double-thick 8-inch square of 100-percent-cotton cheesecloth. Gather corners together and tie closed with 100-percent-cotton kitchen string. Add bouquet garni to slow cooker. Pour broth over all in cooker.

2. Cover and cook on low-heat setting for 7 to 8 hours or on high-heat setting for 3½ to 4 hours. Remove bouquet garni and discard.

3. Using a slotted spoon, transfer chicken to a large bowl, reserving cooking liquid. When chicken is cool enough to handle, remove meat from bones. Using two forks, shred meat. Add enough of the cooking liquid to moisten meat. Strain and reserve cooking liquid to use for chicken stock. Place 2-cup portions of chicken and chicken stock in separate airtight containers. Cover and refrigerate for up to 3 days or freeze for up to 3 months. Thaw in refrigerator before using.

PER SERVING: 115 cal., 4 g total fat (1 g sat. fat), 80 mg chol., 114 mg sodium, 0 g carb. (0 g fiber, 0 g sugars), 19 g pro. Exchanges: 2.5 lean meat.

1

Greek-Style Chicken Salad

13g
CARB PER
SERVING

START TO FINISH: 20 minutes
MAKES: 4 servings (1 salad each)

- **2 cups Shredded Chicken Master Recipe (page 102)**
- **½ cup bottled reduced-calorie Greek vinaigrette salad dressing**
- **1 teaspoon finely shredded lemon peel**
- **½ teaspoon dried oregano, crushed**
- **6 cups torn romaine lettuce**
- **1 medium cucumber, chopped (1⅓ cups)**
- **1 cup grape tomatoes, halved**
- **1 medium yellow sweet pepper, chopped (¾ cup)**
- **1 medium red onion, thinly sliced and separated into rings**
- **½ cup crumbled reduced-fat feta cheese (2 ounces)**
- **¼ cup pitted Kalamata olives, halved**
  Lemon wedges (optional)

1. In a medium bowl combine shredded chicken, ¼ cup of the vinaigrette, the lemon peel, and oregano; set aside.
2. Meanwhile, in a large salad bowl toss lettuce with remaining ¼ cup vinaigrette. Place 1½ cups lettuce in each of four shallow bowls. Top each with ⅓ cup cucumber, ¼ cup tomatoes, 3 tablespoons sweet pepper, and one-fourth of the onion rings. Add ½ cup chicken mixture to the center of each salad. Sprinkle each salad with 2 tablespoons feta cheese and 1 tablespoon olives. If desired, serve with lemon wedges.

PER SERVING: 220 cal., 8 g total fat (3 g sat. fat), 85 mg chol., 481 mg sodium, 13 g carb. (4 g fiber, 5 g sugars), 25 g pro. Exchanges: 2.5 lean meat, 2.5 vegetable, 1 fat.

Apricot-Mustard Chicken Sandwiches

30g
CARB PER
SERVING

START TO FINISH: 15 minutes

MAKES: 4 servings (1 sandwich each)

1 **large onion, finely chopped (1 cup)**

2 **cloves garlic, minced**

1 **tablespoon vegetable oil**

2 **cups Shredded Chicken Master Recipe (page 102)**

3 **tablespoons spicy brown mustard**

3 **tablespoons low-sugar apricot preserves**

1 **tablespoon cider vinegar**

1 **tablespoon bourbon (optional)**

¼ **teaspoon cayenne pepper**

4 **whole wheat hamburger buns, split and toasted**

4 **thin slices red onion (optional)**

1. In a large skillet cook chopped onion and garlic in hot oil over medium heat about 4 minutes or until tender. Stir in shredded chicken, mustard, apricot preserves, vinegar, bourbon (if using), and cayenne pepper. Heat through. If necessary, simmer, uncovered, about 5 minutes or until desired consistency.

2. Spoon about ½ cup chicken mixture onto each bun bottom. If desired, top with red onion slices. Add bun tops.

PER SERVING: 304 cal., 8 g total fat (1 g sat. fat), 80 mg chol., 506 mg sodium, 30 g carb. (3 g fiber, 10 g sugars), 24 g pro. Exchanges: 2 starch, 2.5 lean meat, 1 fat.

Peanut Noodles with Chicken and Vegetables

29 g
CARB PER SERVING

START TO FINISH: 25 minutes
MAKES: 6 servings (1 cup each)

- **6 ounces dried multigrain spaghetti**
- **1 16-ounce package frozen sugar snap stir-fry vegetable blend**
- **1 recipe Peanut Sauce**
- **2 cups Shredded Chicken Master Recipe (page 102)**
- **⅓ cup chopped peanuts and/ or sliced green onions (optional)**

1. In a 4-quart Dutch oven cook spaghetti according to package directions, adding vegetables for the last 2 minutes of cooking time; drain, reserving ¼ cup of the pasta cooking water.

2. Prepare Peanut Sauce. In a large bowl combine pasta mixture, Peanut Sauce, and shredded chicken. Toss well to coat. Serve immediately. If desired, top with chopped peanuts and/or sliced green onions.

Peanut Sauce: In a small saucepan combine 3 tablespoons peanut butter; 1 tablespoon sugar;* 2 tablespoons reduced-sodium soy sauce; 1 tablespoon vegetable oil; 2 cloves garlic, minced; and ¼ teaspoon crushed red pepper. Whisk in the ¼ cup reserved pasta water. Heat until peanut butter is melted and sugar is dissolved, stirring frequently.

*Sugar Substitutes: Choose from Splenda Granular or Sweet'N Low bulk or packets. Follow package directions to use product amount equivalent to 1 tablespoon sugar.

PER SERVING: 289 cal., 9 g total fat (2 g sat. fat), 54 mg chol., 341 mg sodium, 29 g carb. (4 g fiber, 7 g sugars), 21 g pro. Exchanges: 1.5 starch, 2 lean meat, 1 vegetable, 1 fat.

PER SERVING WITH SUBSTITUTE: Same as above, except 282 cal., 27 g carb. (5 g sugars).

Cook Well: Whole grain pasta adds fiber to your diet. Use these tricks for getting the most enjoyment out of these good-for-you noodles:

- Take care not to overcook. Overcooked whole grain pasta can become even mushier than regular pasta.
- Time the cooking of the pasta so that you can toss it with the sauce immediately—this helps keep the pasta moist.
- Once you've tossed the pasta with a sauce, serve it right away. Whole grain pastas will absorb sauces quickly and become dry if you let them stand too long.
- If you're not sure you like the flavor of whole grain pasta, try mixing it with your favorite brand of regular pasta until you get used to its toasty, nutty taste.

Italian Turkey Chili

PREP: 15 minutes **SLOW COOK:** 6 to 8 hours (low) or 3 to 4 hours (high), plus 1 hour (high)
MAKES: 16 servings (1 cup each)

2 **19.2-ounce packages ground turkey breast**

2 **28-ounce cans no-salt-added diced tomatoes, undrained**

2 **15-ounce cans no-salt-added cannellini beans (white kidney beans), rinsed and drained**

½ **cup reduced-sodium chicken broth**

1 **large onion, chopped (1 cup)**

2 **stalks celery, sliced (1 cup)**

1 **medium red or green sweet pepper, chopped (¾ cup)**

1 **6-ounce can no-salt-added tomato paste**

4 **cloves garlic, minced**

2 **teaspoons dried oregano, crushed**

1 **teaspoon fennel seeds**

½ **teaspoon crushed red pepper**

1 **large zucchini, chopped (2 cups)**

2 **cups sliced fresh mushrooms**

2 **tablespoons balsamic vinegar or red wine vinegar**

1. In a large nonstick skillet cook turkey over medium heat until no longer pink, stirring to break apart. Drain. Place in a 5- to 6-quart slow cooker. Add tomatoes, beans, broth, onion, celery, sweet pepper, tomato paste, garlic, fennel seeds, oregano, and crushed red pepper. Stir to combine.

2. Cover and cook on low-heat setting for 6 to 8 hours or on high-heat setting for 3 to 4 hours. If using low-heat setting, turn to high-heat setting. Stir in zucchini and mushrooms. Cover and cook about 1 hour more or until tender. Stir in vinegar.

3. Place 3-cup portions of chili in airtight containers; cover and refrigerate for up to 3 days or freeze for up to 3 months. Thaw in refrigerator before using.

PER SERVING: 158 cal., 1 g total fat (0 g sat. fat), 33 mg chol., 134 mg sodium, 17 g carb. (5 g fiber, 6 g sugars), 20 g pro. Exchanges: 1 starch, 2 lean meat, 1 vegetable.

1

Easy Lasagna

PREP: 30 minutes BAKE: 1 hour 10 minutes STAND: 10 minutes
MAKES: 6 servings (⅙ of the dish each)

1 **15-ounce container fat-free ricotta cheese**

1 **egg**

1 **teaspoon dried Italian seasoning, crushed**

2 **cups shredded fresh spinach**
   Nonstick cooking spray

3 **cups Italian Turkey Chili Master Recipe (page 106)**

6 **sheets no-boil lasagna noodles**

1 **cup shredded part-skim mozzarella cheese (4 ounces)**

1. Preheat oven to 375°F. In a blender or food processor blend ricotta, egg, and Italian seasoning until smooth. Stir in spinach.
2. Coat a 2-quart square baking dish with cooking spray. Spread 1 cup of the turkey chili in the prepared baking dish. Arrange two of the lasagna noodles on chili. Top with one-third of the ricotta cheese mixture. Repeat with two more layers each of chili, lasagna noodles, and cheese mixture.
3. Cover and bake for 1 hour. Sprinkle with mozzarella cheese. Bake, uncovered, about 10 minutes more or until cheese melts. Let stand for 10 minutes before serving.

PER SERVING: 250 cal., 5 g total fat (2 g sat. fat), 93 mg chol., 381 mg sodium, 25 g carb. (3 g fiber, 7 g sugars), 25 g pro. Exchanges: 1.5 starch, 3 lean meat, 0.5 vegetable.

Turkey Chili Spaghetti

33g
CARB PER
SERVING

PREP: 10 minutes **COOK:** 10 minutes

MAKES: 4 servings (½ cup pasta, ¾ cup chili, and about 1½ tablespoons basil mixture each)

- **4 ounces dried multigrain spaghetti**
- **3 cups Italian Turkey Chili Master Recipe (page 106)**
- **¼ cup shredded fresh basil**
- **¼ cup finely shredded Parmesan cheese**
- **2 tablespoons chopped pine nuts, toasted**
- **1 small clove garlic, minced**

1. Prepare spaghetti according to package directions; drain. Meanwhile, in a saucepan heat chili over medium-low heat until heated through. In a small bowl combine the basil, Parmesan, pine nuts, and garlic. Serve chili over hot cooked pasta and sprinkle with basil mixture.

PER SERVING: 275 cal., 6 g total fat (1 g sat. fat), 28 mg chol., 198 mg sodium, 33 g carb. (6 g fiber, 6 g sugars), 23 g pro. Exchanges: 2 starch, 2 lean meat, 0.5 vegetable.

3

Baked Chili Omelet

15g CARB PER SERVING

PREP: 20 minutes **BAKE:** 17 minutes
MAKES: 4 servings (¾ cup chili, ¼ of the omelet, and about 1½ tablespoons garnish each)

Nonstick cooking spray
6 **egg yolks**
½ **teaspoon onion powder**
¼ **teaspoon salt**
⅛ **teaspoon cayenne pepper**
6 **egg whites**
3 **cups Italian Turkey Chili Master Recipe (page 106)**
¼ **cup shredded Parmesan cheese**
2 **tablespoons fresh oregano**

1. Preheat oven to 350°F. Lightly coat a 2-quart square baking dish with cooking spray; set aside.
2. For omelet, in a medium mixing bowl beat egg yolks, onion powder, salt, and cayenne pepper with an electric mixer on medium speed about 4 minutes or until thick and lemon color; set aside.
3. Wash and dry beaters thoroughly. In a large mixing bowl beat egg whites until soft peaks form (tips curl). Gently fold yolk mixture into beaten egg whites. Spread egg mixture evenly in the prepared baking dish.
4. Bake for 17 to 19 minutes or until a knife inserted near the center comes out clean.
5. Meanwhile, in a saucepan heat Italian Turkey Chili over medium-low heat. Cut omelet into four squares; cut each square into two triangles and place on four plates. Top omelet servings with chili. Garnish with Parmesan cheese and oregano.

PER SERVING: 250 cal., 9 g total fat (3 g sat. fat), 305 mg chol., 425 mg sodium, 15 g carb. (4 g fiber, 5 g sugars), 27 g pro. Exchanges: 1 starch, 1 medium-fat meat, 0.5 vegetable.

Pulled Pork

PREP: 30 minutes **SLOW COOK:** 10 to 11 hours (low) or 5 to 6 hours (high)
MAKES: 12 servings (½ cup each)

- 3 **to 3½ pounds boneless pork shoulder roast**
- 1 **medium sweet onion, chopped (1 cup)**
- 1 **cup chili sauce**
- 6 **cloves garlic, minced**
- 2 **tablespoons packed brown sugar***
- 2 **tablespoons cider vinegar**
- 1 **tablespoon Worcestershire sauce**
- 1 **tablespoon chili powder**
- ½ **teaspoon black pepper**

1. Trim fat from roast. If necessary, cut roast to fit in a 4- to 5-quart slow cooker. Place roast and onion in the cooker. In a medium bowl combine chili sauce, garlic, brown sugar, cider vinegar, Worcestershire sauce, chili powder, and pepper. Pour over all in cooker.

2. Cover and cook on low-heat setting for 10 to 11 hours or on high-heat setting for 5 to 6 hours.

3. Remove meat from cooker, reserving cooking liquid. Using two forks, shred meat, discarding fat. Skim fat from liquid. Add enough liquid to the meat to moisten. Place 2-cup portions of pork in airtight containers; cover and refrigerate for up to 3 days or freeze for up to 3 months. Thaw in refrigerator before using.

*Sugar Substitutes: Choose from Sweet'N Low Brown or Sugar Twin Granulated Brown. Follow package directions to use product amount equivalent to 2 tablespoons brown sugar.

PER SERVING: 183 cal., 7 g total fat (2 g sat. fat), 73 mg chol., 360 mg sodium, 6 g carb. (0 g fiber, 5 g sugars), 23 g pro. Exchanges: 0.5 carb., 3 lean meat, 0.5 fat.

PER SERVING WITH SUBSTITUTE: Same as above, except 178 cal., 5 g carb. (4 g sugars). Exchanges: 0 carb.

Cook Well: Here are more ways to turn leftover cooked pork shoulder roast into a meal:

- Pile it into a pita pocket with an assortment of vegetables tossed in reduced-fat dressing.
- Heat it with barbecue sauce and tuck onto a toasted bun. Serve a crisp coleslaw alongside.
- Use it instead of ground beef in chili. Skip the step for browning the meat.
- Tuck it into a Cuban sandwich with thin slices of ham, pickles, mustard, and low-fat Swiss cheese. Add a black bean salad from the deli.

Shredded Pork and Green Chile Roll-Ups

25 g CARB PER SERVING

START TO FINISH: 15 minutes
MAKES: 6 servings (1 roll-up each)

- 1 **large onion, thinly sliced and separated into rings**
- ½ **fresh poblano chile pepper, chopped***
- 2 **teaspoons vegetable oil**
- 2 **cups Pulled Pork Master Recipe (page 110)**
- 6 **8-inch whole wheat flour tortillas, warmed****
- ¾ **cup chopped tomato**
- ½ **cup shredded reduced-fat cheddar cheese (2 ounces)**
- ⅓ **cup light sour cream**
- 3 **tablespoons snipped fresh cilantro**

1. In a large skillet cook onion and poblano pepper in hot oil over medium heat about 5 minutes or until tender, stirring occasionally. Stir in shredded pork. Cook and stir for 2 to 3 minutes or until mixture is heated through.

2. Spoon pork mixture onto each tortilla. Top each with tomato, cheese, sour cream, and cilantro. Roll up tortillas. Cut in half to serve.

***Test Kitchen Tip:** Because chile peppers contain volatile oils that can burn your skin and eyes, avoid direct contact with them as much as possible. When working with chile peppers, wear plastic or rubber gloves. If your bare hands do touch the peppers, wash your hands and nails well with soap and warm water.

****Test Kitchen Tip:** To warm tortillas, wrap in foil and heat in a 350°F oven for 10 minutes.

PER SERVING: 327 cal., 12 g total fat (5 g sat. fat), 58 mg chol., 639 mg sodium, 25 g carb. (11 g fiber, 6 g sugars), 27 g pro. Exchanges: 1.5 starch, 3 lean meat, 0.5 vegetable, 1 fat.

On the Side: Color up your sandwich plate with fresh vegetables. Here are some ideas to add crunch to your lunch or dinner:

- **Sweet peppers:** Offer various colors; slice at least 1 inch thick.
- **Broccoli and cauliflower:** Separate into florets.
- **Jicama:** Peel and slice into ½-inch-wide strips.
- **Cherry tomatoes:** Serve whole.
- **Asparagus:** Trim woody bases. Plunge the spears into boiling water, then into ice water to keep them colorful and crunchy.
- **Carrots and celery:** Serve these sliced into thin sticks.

Mole Pork and Green Olive Quesadillas

28g CARB PER SERVING

PREP: 25 minutes **COOK:** 4 to 6 minutes per batch
MAKES: 6 servings (1 quesadilla each)

Nonstick cooking spray
1 large onion, chopped (1 cup)
3 cloves garlic, minced
2 teaspoons chili powder
½ teaspoon ground cumin
¼ teaspoon ground cinnamon
¼ teaspoon dried oregano, crushed
2 teaspoons flour
⅓ cup water
2 tablespoons semisweet chocolate pieces
2 cups Pulled Pork Master Recipe (page 110)
6 8-inch flour tortillas
¾ cup shredded reduced-fat Monterey Jack cheese (3 ounces)
1 medium red onion, thinly sliced
3 tablespoons sliced pimiento-stuffed green olives

1. Lightly coat an unheated large skillet with cooking spray. Heat over medium heat. Cook onion and garlic about 4 minutes or until tender. Stir in chili powder, cumin, cinnamon, and oregano; cook and stir for 1 minute more. Stir in flour. Stir in the water all at once. Cook and stir until thickened and bubbly. Stir in chocolate until melted. Stir in shredded pork and heat through.

2. Coat one side of each tortilla with cooking spray. Place tortillas, sprayed sides down, on a cutting board or waxed paper. Sprinkle cheese over half of each tortilla. Top evenly with pork mixture, red onion, and green olives. Fold tortillas in half, pressing gently.

3. Preheat oven to 300°F. Heat a large nonstick skillet over medium heat. Cook quesadillas, two at a time, in hot skillet over medium heat for 4 to 6 minutes or until lightly browned, turning once. Remove quesadillas from skillet; place on a baking sheet in oven to keep warm. Repeat with remaining quesadillas. To serve, cut each quesadilla into three wedges.

PER SERVING: 301 cal., 12 g total fat (5 g sat. fat), 59 mg chol., 552 mg sodium, 28 g carb. (2 g fiber, 7 g sugars), 22 g pro. Exchanges: 2 starch, 2 lean meat, 1.5 fat.

Asian Pork and Cabbage Salad

18g
CARB PER SERVING

PREP: 20 minutes **BAKE:** 8 minutes
MAKES: 8 servings (1 cup cabbage, ½ cup meat-vegetable mixture, and ⅛ of the tortilla strips each)

- 3 **8-inch low-carb whole wheat flour tortillas**
- 1 **16-ounce package frozen stir-fry vegetables**
- 1 **tablespoon olive oil**
- 2 **cups Pulled Pork Master Recipe (page 110)**
- ¼ **cup bottled hoisin sauce**
- 1 **teaspoon ground ginger**
- ½ **teaspoon garlic powder**
- 8 **cups shredded or coarsely chopped napa cabbage or bok choy**

1. Preheat oven to 400°F. Cut tortillas into ½-inch-wide strips. Arrange tortilla strips in a single layer on a baking sheet. Bake for 8 to 10 minutes or until lightly browned and crisp. Set aside to cool.
2. In a large skillet cook and stir vegetables in hot oil over medium-high heat for 4 to 5 minutes or until almost tender. Drain off excess liquid. Add pork, hoisin sauce, ginger, and garlic powder to vegetables in skillet. Cook and stir until heated through.
3. Arrange cabbage on eight dinner plates. Spoon meat-vegetable mixture over cabbage. Top with tortilla strips.

PER SERVING: 189 cal., 6 g total fat (2 g sat. fat), 37 mg chol., 422 mg sodium, 18 g carb. (6 g fiber, 8 g sugars), 15 g pro. Exchanges: 1 starch, 1.5 lean meat, 1 vegetable, 0.5 fat.

Cook Well: Hoisin sauce, made from fermented soy beans, garlic, vinegar, sugar, chile peppers, and other seasonings, is a convenient way to add a complex spicy sweetness to recipes—just one ingredient brings a smorgasbord of flavors. Once opened, hoisin sauce should be stored in the refrigerator and used by the "best before" or "use by" date on the bottle.

Shredded Beef

PREP: 30 minutes **SLOW COOK:** 11 to 12 hours (low) or 5½ to 6 hours (high)
MAKES: 12 servings (½ cup each)

3 to 3½ pounds boneless beef chuck pot roast
2 large onions, cut into thin wedges
2 cloves garlic, minced
1 14.5-ounce can lower-sodium beef broth
1 tablespoon Worcestershire sauce
2 teaspoons dry mustard
1 teaspoon dried thyme, crushed
¼ teaspoon salt
¼ teaspoon cayenne pepper

1. Trim fat from roast. If necessary, cut roast to fit into a 4- to 5-quart slow cooker. Place onions and garlic in cooker. Top with roast. In a medium bowl combine broth, Worcestershire sauce, dry mustard, thyme, salt, and cayenne pepper. Pour over all in cooker.
2. Cover and cook on low-heat setting for 11 to 12 hours or on high-heat setting for 5½ to 6 hours.
3. Remove meat from cooker; remove onions with a slotted spoon, reserving cooking liquid. Using two forks, shred meat; discard fat. Skim fat from liquid. Add onions to meat; add enough liquid to the meat to moisten. Place 2-cup portions of meat in airtight containers; cover and refrigerate for up to 3 days or freeze for up to 3 months. Thaw in refrigerator before using.

PER SERVING: 162 cal., 5 g total fat (2 g sat. fat), 50 mg chol., 146 mg sodium, 3 g carb. (0 g fiber, 1 g sugars), 26 g pro. Exchanges: 3.5 lean meat.

Southwestern Shredded Beef Sandwiches

34g
CARB PER SERVING

START TO FINISH: 25 minutes
MAKES: 4 servings (1 sandwich each)

- 1 **large onion, sliced**
- 1 **tablespoon vegetable oil**
- 2 **cups Shredded Beef Master Recipe (page 114)**
- 1 **14.5-ounce can no-salt-added diced tomatoes, undrained**
- 1 **fresh jalapeño chile pepper, seeded and finely chopped***
- 1 **teaspoon ground cumin**
- 1 **teaspoon chili powder**
- 1 **tablespoon chopped fresh cilantro**
- 1 **cup shredded lettuce**
- 4 **whole wheat hamburger buns, split and toasted if desired**
- ½ **cup shredded reduced-fat cheddar or Monterey Jack cheese (2 ounces)**

1. In a large saucepan cook onion in hot oil over medium heat about 4 minutes or until tender. Add shredded beef, tomatoes, jalapeño, cumin, and chili powder. Bring to boiling; reduce heat. Simmer, uncovered, about 5 minutes or until heated through and desired consistency. Stir in cilantro.
2. To serve, divide lettuce among bun bottoms. Spoon about ½ cup meat mixture over lettuce on each bun. Sprinkle with cheese. Add bun tops.

*Test Kitchen Tip: Because chile peppers contain volatile oils that can burn your skin and eyes, avoid direct contact with them as much as possible. When working with chile peppers, wear plastic or rubber gloves. If your bare hands do touch the peppers, wash your hands and nails well with soap and warm water.

PER SERVING: 386 cal., 12 g total fat (4 g sat. fat), 58 mg chol., 511 mg sodium, 34 g carb. (6 g fiber, 10 g sugars), 35 g pro. Exchanges: 2 starch, 4 lean meat, 1 vegetable, 1 fat.

Time-Saving Trick: Toasting sandwich buns helps the bread stand up to the filling and adds crunch to the meal. The easiest way to toast rolls and hoagie buns is in a toaster oven.

You can also use the broiler to toast sandwich rolls and buns. Place the rolls or buns, cut sides up, on the unheated rack of a broiler pan and broil 4 to 5 inches from heat for 1 to 2 minutes or until golden.

Philly Shredded Beef Sandwiches

27 g
CARB PER
SERVING

START TO FINISH: 25 minutes

MAKES: 6 servings (1 sandwich each)

1 **large onion, cut into thin wedges**

2 **cloves garlic, minced**

2 **teaspoons olive oil**

2 **cups Shredded Beef Master Recipe (page 114)**

⅓ **cup lower-sodium beef broth**

3 **bottled pepperoncini salad peppers, stems removed and thinly sliced (optional)**

1 **teaspoon dried oregano, crushed**

1 **teaspoon paprika**

½ **teaspoon black pepper**

¼ **teaspoon celery seeds**

6 **large slices sourdough bread, halved and toasted**

6 **¾-ounce slices reduced-fat Monterey Jack cheese**

2 **tablespoons light mayonnaise**

1. In a large skillet cook onion and garlic in hot oil over medium heat about 5 minutes or until tender. Add shredded beef, broth, pepperoncini peppers (if using), oregano, paprika, black pepper, and celery seeds. Bring to boiling; reduce heat. Simmer, uncovered, about 5 minutes or until heated through and liquid nearly evaporates.

2. Spoon beef mixture over half of the bread slices. Arrange cheese slices on top of beef. Spread mayonnaise on remaining bread slices and place, mayonnaise sides down, on top of cheese.

PER SERVING: 320 cal., 12 g total fat (4 g sat. fat), 50 mg chol., 587 mg sodium, 27 g carb. (2 g fiber, 3 g sugars), 27 g pro. Exchanges: 2 starch, 3 lean meat, 1 fat.

Cook Well: Yeast breads freeze extremely well. Transfer untoasted bread slices or buns to freezer bags and freeze for up to 3 months. Thaw at room temperature.

3

Ropa Vieja

25g
CARB PER SERVING

START TO FINISH: 25 minutes
MAKES: 6 servings (1 cup beef mixture and ⅓ cup rice each)

1 **large onion, cut into thin wedges**
1 **medium green sweet pepper, cut into thin strips**
1 **medium red sweet pepper, cut into thin strips**
3 **cloves garlic, minced**
1 **tablespoon vegetable oil**
2 **cups Shredded Beef Master Recipe (page 114)**
1 **14.5-ounce can no-salt-added diced tomatoes, undrained**
1 **fresh jalapeño chile pepper, seeded and finely chopped* (optional)**
1 **tablespoon red wine vinegar**
1 **teaspoon ground cumin**
¼ **teaspoon black pepper**
2 **cups hot cooked brown rice Fresh jalapeño chile pepper slices* (optional)**

1. In a large skillet cook onion, sweet peppers, and garlic in hot oil over medium-high heat about 5 minutes or until crisp-tender. Add shredded beef, tomatoes, the chopped jalapeño pepper (if using), vinegar, cumin, and black pepper. Bring to boiling; reduce heat. Simmer, uncovered, about 5 minutes or until heated through. Serve over rice. If desired, garnish with jalapeño slices.

*Test Kitchen Tip: Because chile peppers contain volatile oils that can burn your skin and eyes, avoid direct contact with them as much as possible. When working with chile peppers, wear plastic or rubber gloves. If your bare hands do touch the peppers, wash your hands and nails well with soap and warm water.

PER SERVING: 238 cal., 6 g total fat (2 g sat. fat), 33 mg chol., 132 mg sodium, 25 g carb. (4 g fiber, 6 g sugars), 20 g pro. Exchanges: 1 starch, 3 lean meat, 1 vegetable, 1 fat.

Time-Saving Trick:

Cut up the onion, sweet peppers, and garlic the night before and store them in a resealable plastic bag in the refrigerator. When it's time to cook dinner, just empty the contents and cook.

for two

Your mini slow cooker can make mighty-good meals, too! These right-size recipes are perfect when you're cooking just for two and not in the mood for a fridge full of leftovers.

Slow-Cooked Beef with Carrots and Cabbage

14g CARB PER SERVING

PREP: 20 minutes **SLOW COOK:** 7 to 8 hours (low) or 3½ to 4 hours (high), plus 30 minutes (high)
MAKES: 2 servings (3 ounces cooked meat and ¾ cup vegetables each)

8   ounces boneless beef
    chuck pot roast
¼   teaspoon dried
    oregano, crushed
¼   teaspoon ground cumin
¼   teaspoon paprika
¼   teaspoon black pepper
⅛   teaspoon salt
    Nonstick cooking spray
3   medium carrots, cut into
    2-inch pieces
2   small cloves garlic, minced
⅓   cup lower-sodium
    beef broth
2   cups coarsely
    shredded cabbage

1. Trim fat from roast. In a small bowl combine oregano, cumin, paprika, pepper, and salt. Sprinkle mixture evenly over meat; rub in with your fingers. Coat a medium nonstick skillet with cooking spray; heat skillet over medium heat. Add meat to skillet; brown on all sides.
2. Meanwhile, in a 1½- or 2-quart slow cooker combine carrots and garlic. Pour broth over carrots in cooker. Top with meat.
3. Cover and cook on low-heat setting for 7 to 8 hours or on high-heat setting for 3½ to 4 hours. If no heat setting is available, cook for 5 to 5½ hours.
4. If using low-heat setting, turn to high-heat setting (if no heat setting is available, continue cooking). Add cabbage. Cover and cook for 30 minutes more. Using a slotted spoon, transfer meat and vegetables to a serving platter.

PER SERVING: 214 cal., 5 g total fat (2 g sat. fat), 50 mg chol., 379 mg sodium, 14 g carb. (5 g fiber, 7 g sugars), 27 g pro. Exchanges: 3.5 lean meat, 2 vegetable.

Time-Saving Trick: Once you've started the slow cooker, go ahead and coarsely shred the cabbage. Place the shredded cabbage in an airtight container or resealable plastic bag and chill until you need it.

Ultimate Spaghetti and Meatballs

37 g
CARB PER
SERVING

PREP: 25 minutes **SLOW COOK:** 4 to 5 hours (low) or 2 to 2½ hours (high)
MAKES: 2 servings (½ cup cooked spaghetti and 1¼ cups meatball mixture each)

1 cup fresh button or cremini mushrooms, quartered
½ cup thinly sliced sweet onion, such as Vidalia, Maui, or Walla Walla
⅓ cup thin bite-size strips red or yellow sweet pepper
6 1-ounce refrigerated Italian-style cooked turkey meatballs
1 8-ounce can no-salt-added tomato sauce
2 tablespoons no-salt-added tomato paste
1 teaspoon dried Italian seasoning, crushed
2 cloves garlic, minced
1½ ounces dried multigrain spaghetti
Fresh basil leaves (optional)

1. In a 1½- or 2-quart slow cooker combine mushrooms, onion, and sweet pepper. Top with meatballs. In a small bowl combine tomato sauce, tomato paste, Italian seasoning, and garlic. Pour over all in cooker.
2. Cover and cook on low-heat setting for 4 to 5 hours or on high-heat setting for 2 to 2½ hours. If no heat setting is available, cook for 3 to 3½ hours.
3. To serve, cook spaghetti according to package directions; drain. Divide spaghetti between serving plates. Top with meatball mixture. If desired, garnish with basil.

PER SERVING: 357 cal., 12 g total fat (3 g sat. fat), 91 mg chol., 435 mg sodium, 37 g carb. (8 g fiber, 13 g sugars), 25 g pro. Exchanges: 1.5 starch, 2.5 medium-fat meat, 2 vegetable.

Double Tomato-Caper Sauce with Chicken

14g CARB PER SERVING

PREP: 25 minutes **SLOW COOK:** 4 hours (low) or 2 hours (high) **STAND:** 15 minutes
MAKES: 2 servings (1 chicken breast half and ¾ cup sauce each)

1. In a large nonstick skillet cook onion in 1 teaspoon of the oil over medium-high heat about 3 minutes or until soft, stirring frequently. Stir in garlic; cook and stir for 15 seconds. Remove from heat. Stir in sweet pepper, grape tomatoes, dried tomatoes, the water, vinegar, and, if desired, crushed red pepper. Coat an unheated 1½-quart slow cooker with cooking spray. Spoon tomato mixture into the cooker.

2. Cover and cook on low-heat setting for 4 hours or on high-heat setting for 2 hours. If no heat setting is available, cook for 3 hours.

3. Turn off heat. Stir in the remaining oil, the basil, and capers. Cover and let stand for 15 minutes to blend flavors.

4. Meanwhile, coat an unheated large nonstick skillet with nonstick cooking spray. Heat skillet over medium-high heat. Add chicken. Cook for 8 to 10 minutes or until no longer pink (170°F), turning once. Serve sauce over cooked chicken breast.

PER SERVING: 251 cal., 9 g total fat (1 g sat. fat), 66 mg chol., 358 mg sodium, 14 g carb. (4 g fiber, 8 g sugars), 29 g pro. Exchanges: 1 carb., 3.5 lean meat, 1 vegetable, 1 fat.

1 medium onion, chopped (½ cup)
1 tablespoon olive oil
1 clove garlic, minced
½ cup finely chopped red sweet pepper
1 cup grape tomatoes (5 ounces)
½ ounce dried tomatoes (not oil-packed), julienne-cut
2 tablespoons water
1½ teaspoons red wine vinegar
⅛ teaspoon crushed red pepper (optional)
Nonstick cooking spray
2 tablespoons chopped fresh basil
1 tablespoon capers, drained
2 4-ounce skinless, boneless chicken breast halves

Chicken and Cornmeal Dumplings

47g
CARB PER SERVING

PREP: 25 minutes SLOW COOK: 7 to 8 hours (low) or 3½ to 4 hours (high), plus 20 to 25 minutes (high)
MAKES: 2 servings (1½ cups chicken mixture and 2 dumplings each)

2	**medium carrots, thinly sliced (1 cup)**
1	**stalk celery, thinly sliced (½ cup)**
⅓	**cup fresh or frozen whole kernel corn**
½	**of a medium onion, thinly sliced**
2	**cloves garlic, minced**
1	**teaspoon snipped fresh rosemary or ½ teaspoon dried rosemary, crushed**
¼	**teaspoon black pepper**
2	**chicken thighs, skinned**
1	**cup reduced-sodium chicken broth**
½	**cup fat-free milk**
1	**tablespoon flour**
1	**recipe Cornmeal Dumplings**
	Coarsely ground black pepper (optional)

1. In a 1½- or 2-quart slow cooker combine carrots, celery, corn, onion, garlic, rosemary, and the ¼ teaspoon pepper. Top with chicken. Pour broth over all in cooker.
2. Cover and cook on low-heat setting for 7 to 8 hours or on high-heat setting for 3½ to 4 hours. If no heat setting is available, cook for 5 to 5½ hours.
3. If using low-heat setting, turn to high-heat setting (if no heat setting is available, continue cooking). Remove chicken from cooker. Transfer chicken to a cutting board; cool slightly. When cool enough to handle, remove chicken from bones; discard bones. Chop chicken; return to mixture in cooker. In a small bowl whisk or stir milk and flour until smooth. Stir into mixture in cooker.
4. Using two spoons, drop Cornmeal Dumplings dough into four mounds on top of hot chicken mixture. Cover and cook for 20 to 25 minutes more or until a toothpick inserted into a dumpling comes out clean. (Do not lift cover during cooking.) If desired, sprinkle each serving with coarse pepper.

Cornmeal Dumplings: In a medium bowl stir together ¼ cup flour, ¼ cup cornmeal, ½ teaspoon baking powder, and a dash salt. In a small bowl combine 1 egg white, 1 tablespoon fat-free milk, and 1 tablespoon canola oil. Add egg mixture to flour mixture; stir just until moistened.

PER SERVING: 369 cal., 10 g total fat (1 g sat. fat), 55 mg chol., 582 mg sodium, 47 g carb. (5 g fiber, 9 g sugars), 24 g pro. Exchanges: 2.5 starch, 2 lean meat, 1 vegetable, 1 fat.

Time-Saving Trick: Pick up recipe-ready vegetables at a supermarket salad bar. Many will be washed, peeled, and sliced. You will likely pay more per pound for items such as carrots, celery, sweet peppers, broccoli, cauliflower, corn, and onions, but you can buy just the amount you need.

Spicy Drumsticks

3g CARB PER SERVING

PREP: 15 minutes **SLOW COOK:** 6 hours (low) or 3 hours (high) **STAND:** 10 minutes
MAKES: 2 servings (2 drumsticks and 1 teaspoon sauce each)

Nonstick cooking spray
4 chicken drumsticks (about 1 pound total), skinned*
½ cup bottled picante sauce
2 teaspoons bottled cayenne pepper sauce or ⅛ teaspoon cayenne pepper
½ teaspoon smoked paprika
¼ teaspoon dried thyme, crushed
1 bay leaf
2 teaspoons olive oil

1. Lightly coat an unheated 3- or 3½-quart slow cooker with cooking spray. Place chicken in the bottom of the cooker. In a small bowl combine picante sauce, pepper sauce, paprika, thyme, and bay leaf. Spoon over chicken in cooker.
2. Cover and cook on low-heat setting for 6 hours or on high-heat setting for 3 hours.
3. Transfer chicken pieces to a serving bowl. Remove bay leaf from sauce in cooker; stir in the oil. Spoon sauce evenly over the chicken. Cover and let stand for 10 minutes to absorb flavors. To serve, spoon 1 teaspoon sauce over each drumstick. Discard remaining sauce.

***Test Kitchen Tip:** To remove the chicken skin easily, use a paper towel to help grab the skin. If you use your fingers, the skin is very slippery and difficult to hold.

PER SERVING: 209 cal., 9 g total fat (2 g sat. fat), 98 mg chol., 536 mg sodium, 3 g carb. (0 g fiber, 2 g sugars), 27 g pro. Exchanges: 4 lean meat.

On the Side: Round out your meal of these finger-lickin'-good drumsticks with cooked brown rice or Spanish-style rice and steamed green beans.

Veggie-Stuffed Potatoes

PREP: 20 minutes **SLOW COOK:** 7 to 8 hours (low) or 3½ to 4 hours (high)
MAKES: 2 servings (1 potato, ¾ cup vegetables, 2 tablespoons sour cream, 2 tablespoons feta, and 1 tablespoon pine nuts each)

1. Scrub potatoes; pat dry. Prick potatoes; wrap each in foil. Place potatoes in a 3½- or 4-quart slow cooker. Cover and cook on low-heat setting for 4 hours or on high-heat setting for 2 hours.
2. Fold a 24x18-inch sheet of heavy foil in half to form an 18×12-inch rectangle. In a medium bowl combine sweet pepper, onion, zucchini, oil, oregano, and black pepper; place mixture in center of foil. Bring up long sides of foil and fold to seal. Roll up short sides of foil to completely enclose vegetables, leaving space for steam to build. Place foil packet on top of potatoes in cooker.
3. Cover and cook on low-heat setting for 3 to 4 hours longer or on high-heat setting for 1½ to 2 hours longer.
4. Remove foil packet and potatoes from cooker. Unwrap potatoes. Cut potatoes in half lengthwise, cutting to but not through the bottoms. Fluff potatoes. Top potatoes with sour cream and vegetables; sprinkle with salt. Sprinkle with feta cheese and pine nuts.

PER SERVING: 306 cal., 11 g total fat (3 g sat. fat), 8 mg chol., 419 mg sodium, 44 g carb. (5 g fiber, 7 g sugars), 11 g pro. Exchanges: 2.5 starch, 0.5 lean meat, 1 vegetable, 1.5 fat.

2 baking potatoes (6 ounces each)
½ of a medium red sweet pepper, cut into ¾-inch pieces
½ of a medium onion, cut into ½-inch wedges
½ of a medium zucchini or yellow squash, cut into ¾-inch cubes
1 teaspoon olive oil
½ teaspoon dried oregano, crushed
⅛ teaspoon black pepper
¼ cup fat-free sour cream
⅛ teaspoon salt
¼ cup crumbled reduced-fat or fat-free feta cheese
2 tablespoons pine nuts, toasted

Cheesy Ham and Veggie Bowls

37 g
CARB PER
SERVING

PREP: 15 minutes **SLOW COOK:** 6 to 7 hours (low) or 3 to 3½ hours (high) **STAND:** 10 minutes
MAKES: 2 servings (1½ cups each)

1 **small zucchini, chopped (1½ cups)**

1½ **cups frozen whole kernel corn**

1 **red sweet pepper, chopped (¾ cup)**

½ **medium fresh poblano chile pepper, seeded and thinly sliced***

1½ **ounces reduced-sodium ham, chopped**

½ **teaspoon smoked paprika**

2 **tablespoons water**

⅓ **cup thinly sliced green onions**

¼ **cup shredded reduced-fat cheddar cheese (1 ounce)**

2 **tablespoons snipped fresh cilantro or parsley**

1 **tablespoon fat-free milk**

2 **tablespoons shredded reduced-fat cheddar cheese**

1. In a 2-quart slow cooker combine zucchini, corn, sweet pepper, poblano pepper, ham, and paprika. Drizzle the water over mixture in cooker.

2. Cover and cook on low-heat setting for 6 to 7 hours or on high-heat setting for 3 to 3½ hours. Stir in green onions, ¼ cup cheese, the cilantro, and milk. Remove liner from cooker. Let stand, covered, for 10 minutes. Serve in bowls; top with remaining cheese.

***Test Kitchen Tip:** Because chile peppers contain volatile oils that can burn your skin and eyes, avoid direct contact with them as much as possible. When working with chile peppers, wear plastic or rubber gloves. If your bare hands do touch the peppers, wash your hands and nails well with soap and warm water.

PER SERVING: 251 cal., 7 g total fat (4 g sat. fat), 26 mg chol., 364 mg sodium, 37 g carb. (5 g fiber, 9 g sugars), 16 g pro. Exchanges: 2 starch, 1.5 lean meat, 1 vegetable.

Citrus Salmon Fillets with Raspberry Salsa

9g CARB PER SERVING

PREP: 20 minutes **SLOW COOK:** 2½ hours to 3 hours (low) or 1½ hours (high)
MAKES: 2 servings (4 ounces cooked salmon and about ½ cup salsa each)

Nonstick cooking spray
¼ cup water
4 ½-inch-thick orange slices
2 6-ounce salmon fillets with skin on
1 teaspoon canola oil
¼ teaspoon dried tarragon leaves, crushed
¼ teaspoon salt
¼ teaspoon coarsely ground black pepper
1 recipe Raspberry Salsa
1 small lemon, quartered

1. Lightly coat an unheated 1½-quart slow cooker with variable heat settings with cooking spray. Pour the water into the slow cooker. Place orange slices in bottom of cooker, overlapping slightly if necessary. Rinse salmon fillets and pat dry. Place salmon, skin sides down, on top of orange slices; drizzle oil evenly over the fillets. Sprinkle evenly with tarragon, salt, and black pepper.

2. Cover and cook on low-heat setting for 2½ to 3 hours or on high-heat setting for 1½ hours or until salmon is opaque in center.

3. Using a flat spatula, carefully remove salmon and place on dinner plates. Discard oranges and cooking liquid in cooker. Serve salmon with Raspberry Salsa and lemon wedges.

Raspberry Salsa: In a small bowl combine ¼ teaspoon finely shredded orange peel; ¼ cup diced orange sections; ½ of a fresh medium jalapeño chile pepper, seeded and finely chopped*; and 1 tablespoon finely chopped red onion. Toss gently until combined. Fold in ½ cup fresh raspberries and let stand about 15 minutes to blend flavors.

*Test Kitchen Tip: Because chile peppers contain volatile oils that can burn your skin and eyes, avoid direct contact with them as much as possible. When working with chile peppers, wear plastic or rubber gloves. If your bare hands do touch the peppers, wash your hands and nails well with soap and warm water.

PER SERVING: 296 cal., 13 g total fat (2 g sat. fat), 94 mg chol., 367 mg sodium, 9 g carb. (3 g fiber, 4 g sugars), 35 g pro. Exchanges: 0.5 fruit, 5 lean meat, 1 fat.

saucy pasta

With just a few tweaks, hearty pasta takes a healthful turn in these recipes. Find Beef Stroganoff, Coq au Vin, Cheesy Vegetable Alfredo, Hungarian Pork Goulash, and other nutritious, slow-cooked-to-perfection recipes everyone will enjoy.

Herbed Chicken and Mushrooms

29g CARB PER SERVING

PREP: 25 minutes **SLOW COOK:** 7 to 8 hours (low) or 3½ to 4 hours (high)
MAKES: 6 servings (2 chicken thighs, ⅔ cup vegetable mixture, and ½ cup cooked noodles each)

5 cups sliced assorted fresh mushrooms
1 medium onion, chopped
1 medium carrot, chopped
¼ cup dried tomato pieces (not oil-packed)
¾ cup reduced-sodium chicken broth
¼ cup dry white wine or reduced-sodium chicken broth
3 tablespoons quick-cooking tapioca, crushed
1 teaspoon dried thyme, crushed
½ teaspoon dried basil, crushed
½ teaspoon salt
¼ to ½ teaspoon black pepper
12 small chicken thighs and/or drumsticks (about 3 pounds total), skinned
3 cups hot cooked whole wheat and/or spinach fettuccine Small fresh basil leaves (optional)

1. In a 4- to 5-quart slow cooker combine mushrooms, onion, carrot, and dried tomato pieces. Add chicken broth and wine. Sprinkle with tapioca, thyme, dried basil, salt, and pepper. Add chicken pieces to cooker.
2. Cover and cook on low-heat setting for 7 to 8 hours or on high-heat setting for 3½ to 4 hours.
3. Transfer chicken and vegetables to a serving platter. Spoon some of the cooking liquid over the top. Serve with hot cooked pasta. If desired, garnish with fresh basil.

PER SERVING: 306 cal., 7 g total fat (2 g sat. fat), 107 mg chol., 415 mg sodium, 29 g carb. (5 g fiber, 4 g sugars), 33 g pro. Exchanges: 1.5 starch, 4 lean meat, 1 vegetable.

Cook Well: When a recipe calls for chicken broth, use your homemade recipe or choose one of these convenient options:
- Canned broth: Reach for reduced-sodium broth. If you have extra, refrigerate the broth up to 3 days or freeze up to 2 months.
- Bouillon: Instant bouillon granules or cubes are especially handy when you need small amounts of broth for a recipe. Mix 1 teaspoon or 1 small cube with 1 cup water. Choose low-sodium varieties.

Coq au Vin

PREP: 35 minutes **SLOW COOK:** 5 to 5½ hours (low) or 2½ to 2¾ hours (high)
MAKES: 6 servings (1 chicken thigh, ½ cup noodles, and ¾ cup vegetable mixture each)

1. In a 4- to 5-quart slow cooker combine mushrooms, carrots, and onions. Set aside.
2. Lightly coat an unheated large nonstick skillet with cooking spray; heat over medium-high heat. Sprinkle both sides of chicken thighs with ¼ teaspoon of the salt and ¼ teaspoon of the pepper. Add chicken thighs to skillet, meaty sides down. Cook about 6 minutes or until browned, turning once. Add chicken to cooker.
3. Add wine to skillet; bring to boiling. Reduce heat; simmer for 2 minutes, using a wooden spoon to scrape up browned bits from bottom and sides of skillet. Remove from heat. Stir in broth, tapioca, vinegar, herbes de Provence, garlic, the remaining ¼ teaspoon salt, and the remaining ¼ teaspoon pepper. Pour over chicken in cooker.
4. Cover and cook on low-heat setting for 5 to 5½ hours or on high-heat setting for 2½ to 2¾ hours. To serve, sprinkle with parsley and serve with noodles.

PER SERVING: 295 cal., 5 g total fat (1 g sat. fat), 80 mg chol., 365 mg sodium, 33 g carb. (5 g fiber, 5 g sugars), 25 g pro. Exchanges: 2 starch, 2.5 lean meat, 1 vegetable.

Ingredients:

- 1 8-ounce package fresh mushrooms, halved (or quartered if large)
- 4 medium carrots, cut into ¼-inch slices
- 1½ cups frozen pearl onions
  Nonstick cooking spray
- 6 chicken thighs, skinned (2¼ to 2½ pounds total)
- ½ teaspoon salt
- ½ teaspoon black pepper
- 1 cup dry red wine or reduced-sodium chicken broth
- ½ cup reduced-sodium chicken broth
- 2 tablespoons tapioca, crushed
- 2 tablespoons red wine vinegar
- 1½ teaspoons herbes de Provence
- 3 cloves garlic, minced
- 2 tablespoons snipped fresh Italian (flat-leaf) parsley
- 3 cups hot cooked whole grain wide noodles

Time-Saving Trick: Browning and draining meat before adding it to the slow cooker takes a few minutes, but doing so gives color and flavor to the dish and helps remove excess fat.

To save time, use a skillet that's large enough to brown the meat in one batch. If your skillet cannot hold the meat in one layer, you'll have to brown the meat in two batches because overcrowded meat steams rather than browns. If you cook large-batch recipes often, splurge on an extra-large skillet.

Chicken Osso Buco

33g CARB PER SERVING

PREP: 45 minutes **SLOW COOK:** 5 to 6 hours (low) or 2½ to 3 hours (high)
MAKES: 6 servings (2 drumsticks, ⅔ cup sauce, and ½ cup pasta each)

2 tablespoons flour
½ teaspoon salt
¼ teaspoon black pepper
12 medium chicken drumsticks (about 3 pounds total), skinned
1 tablespoon olive oil
2 medium carrots, chopped (1 cup)
1 large onion, chopped (1 cup)
2 stalks celery, sliced (1 cup)
6 cloves garlic, minced
2 tablespoons quick-cooking tapioca, crushed
1 8-ounce can tomato sauce
½ cup dry white wine or reduced-sodium chicken broth
¼ cup reduced-sodium chicken broth
1 teaspoon finely shredded lemon peel
1 tablespoon lemon juice
1 teaspoon dried thyme, crushed
3 cups hot cooked multigrain penne pasta

1. Place flour, salt, and pepper in a resealable plastic bag. Add chicken, a few pieces at time, shaking to coat. In a large skillet brown chicken, half at a time, in hot oil over medium heat about 10 minutes or until golden, turning once.
2. In a 4- to 5-quart slow cooker combine carrots, onion, celery, and garlic. Sprinkle with tapioca. Place chicken on top of vegetables. In a medium bowl stir together tomato sauce, wine, broth, lemon peel, lemon juice, and thyme; pour over all in cooker.
3. Cover and cook on low-heat setting for 5 to 6 hours or on high-heat setting for 2½ to 3 hours. Serve chicken and sauce over hot cooked pasta.

PER SERVING: 345 cal., 7 g total fat (1 g sat. fat), 98 mg chol., 522 mg sodium, 33 g carb. (4 g fiber, 4 g sugars), 33 g pro. Exchanges: 1.5 starch, 4 lean meat, 1 vegetable, 0.5 fat.

Veggies, Turkey, and Pasta

36g CARB PER SERVING

PREP: 40 minutes **SLOW COOK:** 7 to 8 hours (low) or 3½ to 4 hours (high)
MAKES: 8 servings (1⅓ cups each)

1. In an extra-large skillet cook turkey in hot oil until lightly browned on all sides.
2. In a 4- to 5-quart slow cooker stir together tomatoes and soup. Stir in the browned turkey, carrots, celery, onions, garlic, Italian seasoning, salt, and pepper.
3. Cover and cook on low-heat setting for 7 to 8 hours or on high-heat setting for 3½ to 4 hours.
4. Meanwhile, cook penne pasta according to package directions; drain. Gently stir penne into cooker. Serve in shallow bowls and sprinkle each serving with cheese.

PER SERVING: 260 cal., 4 g total fat (1 g sat. fat), 38 mg chol., 440 mg sodium, 36 g carb. (4 g fiber, 7 g sugars), 20 g pro. Exchanges: 2 starch, 2 lean meat, 1.5 vegetable.

- 1 pound turkey breast tenderloin, cut into ¾-inch cubes
- 2 teaspoons olive oil
- 2 14.5-ounce cans no-salt-added diced tomatoes, undrained
- 1 10.75-ounce can reduced-fat and reduced-sodium condensed cream of mushroom soup
- 4 medium carrots, sliced (2 cups)
- 3 stalks celery, sliced (1½ cups)
- 3 medium onions, chopped (1½ cups)
- 4 cloves garlic, minced
- 2 teaspoons dried Italian seasoning, crushed
- ½ teaspoon salt
- ¼ teaspoon black pepper
- 8 ounces dried multigrain penne pasta
- ¼ cup shredded reduced-fat cheddar cheese (1 ounce)

Mediterranean Beef with Pasta

PREP: 25 minutes **SLOW COOK:** 7 to 9 hours (low) or 3½ to 4½ hours (high), plus 30 minutes (high)
MAKES: 6 servings (1 cup beef-vegetable mixture and ⅔ cup pasta each)

1. In a large skillet heat oil over medium-high heat. Add half of the meat; cook and stir until browned. Place meat in a 3½- or 4-quart slow cooker. Repeat with remaining meat. Add carrots, onion, and sweet pepper to cooker. Sprinkle with Italian seasoning, garlic, salt, and black pepper. Pour tomatoes and broth over meat and vegetables in cooker.
2. Cover and cook on low-heat setting for 7 to 9 hours or on high-heat setting for 3½ to 4½ hours.
3. If using low-heat setting, turn to high-heat setting. Stir in zucchini. Cover and cook for 30 minutes more. Meanwhile, cook pasta according to package directions; drain.
4. Serve meat and vegetable mixture over pasta. Sprinkle with Basil Gremolata.

Basil Gremolata: In a small bowl stir together 2 tablespoons finely shredded Parmesan cheese, 2 tablespoons snipped basil, and 2 cloves garlic, minced.

PER SERVING: 354 cal., 11 g total fat (4 g sat. fat), 62 mg chol., 403 mg sodium, 31 g carb. (5 g fiber, 7 g sugars), 32 g pro. Exchanges: 1.5 starch, 3.5 lean meat, 1 vegetable, 1 fat.

1   tablespoon olive oil
1½ pounds lean beef stew meat, cut into 1-inch pieces and trimmed of fat
3   medium carrots, cut into ½-inch slices
1   medium onion, cut into thin wedges
1   medium yellow sweet pepper, cut into 1-inch pieces
1   teaspoon dried Italian seasoning, crushed
2   cloves garlic, minced
¼   teaspoon salt
¼   teaspoon black pepper
1   14.5-ounce can diced tomatoes, undrained
½   cup lower-sodium beef broth
1   medium zucchini, halved lengthwise and cut into ¼-inch-thick slices
6   ounces dried multigrain or whole grain penne pasta
1   recipe Basil Gremolata

So-Easy Pepper Steak

31g
CARB PER
SERVING

PREP: 15 minutes   **SLOW COOK:** 9 to 10 hours (low) or 4½ to 5 hours (high)
MAKES: 6 servings (4 ounces cooked meat, ¾ cup vegetable and sauce mixture, and ½ cup cooked pasta each)

2 **pounds boneless beef round steak, cut ¾ to 1 inch thick**
½ **teaspoon salt**
¼ **teaspoon black pepper**
1 **14.5-ounce can Cajun-, Mexican-, or Italian-style stewed tomatoes, undrained**
½ **of a 6-ounce can (⅓ cup) no-salt-added tomato paste**
½ **teaspoon bottled hot pepper sauce (optional)**
1 **16-ounce package frozen peppers and onions stir-fry vegetables**
3 **cups hot cooked whole wheat pasta**

1. Trim fat from meat. Cut meat into six serving-size portions. Sprinkle meat with the salt and black pepper. Place meat in a 3½- or 4-quart slow cooker.
2. In a medium bowl combine tomatoes, tomato paste, and, if desired, hot pepper sauce. Pour over meat in cooker. Top with frozen vegetables.
3. Cover and cook on low-heat setting for 9 to 10 hours or on high-heat setting for 4½ to 5 hours. Serve over hot cooked pasta.

PER SERVING: 348 cal., 8 g total fat (3 g sat. fat), 91 mg chol., 544 mg sodium, 31 g carb. (6 g fiber, 5 g sugars), 38 g pro. Exchanges: 1.5 starch, 4.5 lean meat, 1 vegetable.

On the Side: Toss together a salad of fresh baby spinach leaves, sliced fresh mushrooms, slivers of red onion, and a little balsamic vinaigrette to serve with this classic family-style dinner.

Beef Stroganoff

22g CARB PER SERVING

1½ **pounds beef stew meat**

2 **teaspoons vegetable oil**
2 **cups sliced fresh mushrooms**
1 **medium onion, chopped (½ cup)**
2 **cloves garlic, minced**
½ **teaspoon dried oregano, crushed**
½ **teaspoon salt**
¼ **teaspoon dried thyme, crushed**
¼ **teaspoon black pepper**
1 **bay leaf**
1 **14.5-ounce can lower-sodium beef broth**
⅓ **cup dry sherry or lower-sodium beef broth**
1 **8-ounce carton light sour cream**
2 **tablespoons cornstarch**
2 **cups hot cooked noodles Snipped fresh parsley (optional)**

1. Trim fat from beef. Cut beef into 1-inch pieces. In a large skillet cook beef, half at a time, in hot oil over medium heat until browned. Drain off fat.
2. In a 3½- or 4-quart slow cooker place mushrooms, onion, garlic, oregano, salt, thyme, pepper, and bay leaf. Add beef. Pour broth and sherry over all in cooker.
3. Cover and cook on low-heat setting for 8 to 10 hours or on high-heat setting for 4 to 5 hours. Discard bay leaf.
4. If using low-heat setting, turn to high-heat setting. In a medium bowl combine sour cream and cornstarch. Gradually whisk about 1 cup of the hot cooking liquid into sour cream mixture. Stir sour cream mixture into cooker. Cover and cook about 30 minutes more or until thickened. Serve over hot cooked noodles. If desired, sprinkle each serving with parsley.

PER SERVING: 342 cal., 12 g total fat (4 g sat. fat), 89 mg chol., 441 mg sodium, 22 g carb. (1 g fiber, 4 g sugars), 32 g pro. Exchanges: 1 starch, 4 lean meat, 1 vegetable, 1 fat.

Greek Lamb with Spinach and Orzo

28g CARB PER SERVING

PREP: 25 minutes **SLOW COOK:** 8 to 10 hours (low) or 4 to 5 hours (high)
MAKES: 10 servings (1 cup lamb mixture, 1 cup spinach, and 1½ tablespoons cheese each)

1. In a small bowl stir together oregano, lemon peel, garlic, and salt. Sprinkle oregano mixture evenly over lamb; rub in with your fingers. Place lamb in a 3½- or 4-quart slow cooker. Sprinkle lamb with lemon juice.
2. Cover and cook on low-heat setting for 8 to 10 hours or on high-heat setting for 4 to 5 hours.
3. Meanwhile, cook orzo according to package directions; drain. Stir cooked orzo into meat mixture in cooker. Place spinach on a large serving platter. Spoon lamb mixture over spinach. Sprinkle with feta cheese. Serve with lemon wedges.

PER SERVING: 347 cal., 10 g total fat (4 g sat. fat), 92 mg chol., 417 mg sodium, 28 g carb. (2 g fiber, 1 g sugars), 36 g pro. Exchanges: 1.5 starch, 4 lean meat, 1 vegetable.

- 1 tablespoon dried oregano, crushed
- 1 tablespoon finely shredded lemon peel
- 4 cloves garlic, minced
- ½ teaspoon salt
- 3 pounds lamb stew meat
- ¼ cup lemon juice
- 12 ounces dried orzo (2 cups dried)
- 1 10-ounce package fresh spinach, chopped
- 1 cup crumbled reduced-fat feta cheese (4 ounces)
  Lemon wedges

Hungarian Pork Goulash

24g CARB PER SERVING

PREP: 30 minutes **SLOW COOK:** 5 to 6 hours (low) or 2½ to 3 hours (high), plus 30 minutes (high)
MAKES: 6 servings (1¼ cups each)

1 1½- to 2-pound pork sirloin roast
1 tablespoon Hungarian paprika or Spanish paprika
1 teaspoon caraway seeds, crushed
½ teaspoon garlic powder
½ teaspoon black pepper
¼ teaspoon salt
1 tablespoon canola oil
2 stalks celery, thinly sliced (1 cup)
2 medium carrots, thinly sliced (1 cup)
2 medium parsnips, halved lengthwise if large and thinly sliced (1 cup)
1 large onion, chopped (1 cup)
1 14.5-ounce can no-salt-added diced tomatoes, undrained
½ cup water
4 ounces dried wide whole grain noodles (2 cups dried)
6 tablespoons light sour cream
Paprika (optional)

1. Trim fat from roast. Cut roast into 2-inch cubes. In a large bowl combine paprika, caraway seeds, garlic powder, pepper, and salt. Add pork cubes and toss to coat. In a large skillet cook pork, half at a time, in hot oil over medium heat until browned, turning occasionally. Transfer pork to a 3½- or 4-quart slow cooker. Add celery, carrots, parsnips, onion, and tomatoes. Pour the water over all in cooker.

2. Cover and cook on low-heat setting for 5 to 6 hours or on high-heat setting for 2½ to 3 hours.

3. If using low-heat setting, turn to high-heat setting. Stir noodles into pork mixture in cooker. Cover and cook on high-heat setting for 30 minutes more or until noodles are tender, stirring once halfway through cooking. Top each serving with 1 tablespoon sour cream. If desired, sprinkle each serving with additional paprika.

PER SERVING: 285 cal., 9 g total fat (2 g sat. fat), 82 mg chol., 234 mg sodium, 24 g carb. (5 g fiber, 6 g sugars), 28 g pro. Exchanges: 1 starch, 3 lean meat, 2 vegetable, 1 fat.

Cajun-Style Pork and Shrimp Pasta

35g CARB PER SERVING

PREP: 30 minutes **SLOW COOK:** 6 to 7 hours (low) or 3 to 3½ hours (high), plus 15 minutes (high)
MAKES: 8 servings (1½ cups each)

1. Trim fat from roast. Cut roast into three portions. Sprinkle pork portions with salt and black pepper. Coat an unheated large nonstick skillet with cooking spray; heat over medium heat. Brown roast portions in hot skillet, turning to brown all sides evenly. In a 3½- or 4-quart slow cooker combine celery, onion, beans, and tomatoes. Top with browned pork pieces.
2. Cover and cook on low-heat setting for 6 to 7 hours or on high-heat setting for 3 to 3½ hours.
3. Meanwhile, cook pasta according to package directions, except cook 1 minute less than package directions; drain. Remove meat from cooker; set aside. If using low-heat setting, turn to high-heat setting. Add Cajun seasoning, pasta, and sweet pepper to the cooker. Cover and cook for 15 minutes more. Cut meat into ½- to ¾-inch cubes; stir into pasta mixture along with thawed shrimp. Sprinkle each serving with cilantro.

Homemade Salt-Free Cajun Seasoning: In a small bowl stir together 1 teaspoon onion powder, 1 teaspoon paprika, ¾ teaspoon ground white pepper, ¾ teaspoon garlic powder, ¼ teaspoon cayenne pepper, and ¼ teaspoon black pepper.

PER SERVING: 306 cal., 5 g total fat (1 g sat. fat), 109 mg chol., 370 mg sodium, 35 g carb. (6 g fiber, 4 g sugars), 32 g pro. Exchanges: 2 starch, 3.5 lean meat, 1 vegetable.

1   1½- to 2-pound pork sirloin roast
½   teaspoon salt
¼   teaspoon black pepper
    Nonstick cooking spray
2   stalks celery, thinly sliced (1 cup)
1   large onion, cut into thin wedges
1   15-ounce can red beans, rinsed and drained
1   14.5-ounce can no-salt-added diced tomatoes, undrained
8   ounces dried multigrain rotini pasta (3¼ cups dried)
1½ tablespoons salt-free Cajun seasoning or Homemade Salt-Free Cajun Seasoning
1   medium green sweet pepper, chopped (¾ cup)
8   ounces frozen peeled and deveined cooked shrimp, thawed
    Snipped fresh cilantro

Mediterranean Shrimp and Pasta

32g CARB PER SERVING

PREP: 25 minutes **SLOW COOK:** 4 hours (low) or 2 hours (high), plus 30 minutes (high)
MAKES: 4 servings (¾ cup shrimp mixture and ½ cup pasta each)

8 ounces fresh or frozen medium shrimp
  Nonstick cooking spray
1 14.5-ounce can no-salt-added diced tomatoes, drained
1 cup sliced zucchini
1 large red sweet pepper, chopped (1 cup)
½ cup dry white wine or reduced-sodium chicken broth
2 cloves garlic, minced
8 pitted Kalamata olives, chopped
¼ cup chopped fresh basil
1 tablespoon olive oil
1½ teaspoons chopped fresh rosemary or ½ teaspoon dried rosemary, crushed
¼ teaspoon salt
4 ounces dried acini di pepe or whole wheat acini di pepe, cooked according to package directions
2 ounces reduced-fat feta cheese, crumbled

1. Thaw shrimp, if frozen. Peel and devein shrimp; cover and chill until ready to use. Lightly coat an unheated 1½-quart slow cooker with cooking spray. In the slow cooker combine tomatoes, zucchini, sweet pepper, wine, and garlic.

2. Cover and cook on low-heat setting for 4 hours or high-heat setting for 2 hours. (If no heat setting is available, cook for 3 hours.) Stir in the shrimp. If using low-heat setting, turn to high-heat setting. Cover and cook for 30 minutes more.

3. Stir in olives, basil, olive oil, rosemary, and salt. Place cooked pasta in a serving bowl and top with shrimp mixture. Sprinkle feta cheese evenly over all.

PER SERVING: 302 cal., 8 g total fat (2 g sat. fat), 90 mg chol., 572 mg sodium, 32 g carb. (4 g fiber, 6 g sugars), 20 g pro. Exchanges: 1.5 starch, 2 lean meat, 2 vegetable, 1 fat.

Pasta with Marinara Sauce

35g CARB PER SERVING

PREP: 20 minutes **SLOW COOK:** 8 to 10 hours (low) or 4 to 5 hours (high)
MAKES: 8 servings (½ cup spaghetti and ¾ cup sauce each)

1. In a 3½- or 4-quart slow cooker combine tomatoes, carrots, celery, onion, sweet peppers, tomato paste, the water, sugar (if using), Italian seasoning, garlic, salt, black pepper, and bay leaf.
2. Cover and cook on low-heat setting for 8 to 10 hours or on high-heat setting for 4 to 5 hours.
3. Stir in sugar substitute, if using. Discard bay leaf. Serve sauce over hot cooked pasta. Sprinkle with cheese.

*Sugar Substitutes: Choose from Splenda Granular or Sweet'N Low bulk or packets. Follow package directions to use product amount equivalent to 2 teaspoons sugar. Stir in sugar substitute after cooking.

PER SERVING: 188 cal., 2 g total fat (1 g sat. fat), 2 mg chol., 401 mg sodium, 35 g carb. (6 g fiber, 10 g sugars), 9 g pro. Exchanges: 2 starch, 1.5 vegetable.

PER SERVING WITH SUBSTITUTE: Same as above, except 185 cal., 34 g carb. (9 g sugars).

- 1 **28-ounce can whole Italian-style tomatoes, cut up and undrained**
- 4 **medium carrots, coarsely chopped (2 cups)**
- 3 **stalks celery, sliced (1½ cups)**
- 1 **large onion, chopped (1 cup)**
- 2 **small green sweet peppers, chopped (1 cup)**
- 1 **6-ounce can no-salt-added tomato paste**
- ½ **cup water**
- 2 **teaspoons sugar***
- 2 **teaspoons dried Italian seasoning, crushed**
- 3 **cloves garlic, minced**
- ½ **teaspoon salt**
- ¼ **teaspoon black pepper**
- 1 **bay leaf**
- 4 **cups hot cooked whole grain spaghetti (8 ounces dried)**
- 1 **ounce Parmesan cheese, shaved into shards**

Cheesy Vegetable Alfredo

39g CARB PER SERVING

PREP: 25 minutes **SLOW COOK:** 5 to 5½ hours (low) or 2 to 2½ hours (high) **STAND:** 5 minutes
MAKES: 6 servings (1½ cups each)

8 ounces fresh green beans, trimmed and halved crosswise

2 cups fresh button or cremini mushrooms, sliced

½ of a medium head cauliflower, cut into large florets

1 9-ounce package frozen artichoke hearts, thawed

2 medium carrots, thinly sliced (1 cup)

1 medium onion, chopped (1 cup)

1 cup fat-free evaporated milk

1 5- to 6.5-ounce container light semisoft cheese with garlic and fine herbs

1 cup shredded Parmesan cheese (4 ounces)

6 ounces dried whole grain linguine

1 cup cherry tomatoes, quartered or halved
Shredded fresh basil

1. In a 4- to 5-quart slow cooker combine green beans, mushrooms, cauliflower, artichoke hearts, carrots, and onion. Pour evaporated milk over all in cooker.

2. Cover and cook on low-heat setting for 5 to 5½ hours or on high-heat setting for 2 to 2½ hours.

3. Add semisoft cheese and Parmesan cheese to cooker. Cover and let stand for 5 minutes. Stir gently until cheese melts. Meanwhile, cook linguine according to package directions; drain. Add linguine to cooker and toss to coat. Divide pasta mixture among six serving plates. Top each serving with tomatoes and basil.

PER SERVING: 343 cal., 11 g total fat (7 g sat. fat), 31 mg chol., 547 mg sodium, 39 g carb. (9 g fiber, 8 g sugars), 19 g pro. Exchanges: 2 starch, 2 lean meat, 1 vegetable, 1.5 fat.

Pasta with Eggplant Sauce

PREP: 25 minutes **SLOW COOK:** 7 to 8 hours (low) or 3½ to 4 hours (high)
MAKES: 8 servings (¾ cup sauce, ½ cup pasta, and ½ tablespoon cheese each)

1. Peel eggplant, if desired; cut eggplant into 1-inch pieces. In a 3½- to 5-quart slow cooker stir together eggplant, tomatoes, tomato paste, mushrooms, onion, wine, the water, oregano, and garlic.
2. Cover and cook on low-heat setting for 7 to 8 hours or on high-heat setting for 3½ to 4 hours.
3. Stir in olives and parsley. Season to taste with pepper. Serve over pasta. Top with Parmesan cheese and, if desired, pine nuts.

PER SERVING: 203 cal., 3 g total fat (0 g sat. fat), 2 mg chol., 413 mg sodium, 36 g carb. (7 g fiber, 7 g sugars), 9 g pro. Exchanges: 1.5 starch, 1.5 vegetable, 0.5 fat.

1 **medium eggplant**
2 **14.5-ounce cans no-salt-added diced tomatoes, undrained**
1 **6-ounce can Italian-style tomato paste**
1 **4-ounce can (drained weight) sliced mushrooms, drained**
1 **medium onion, chopped (½ cup)**
¼ **cup dry red wine**
¼ **cup water**
1¼ **teaspoons dried oregano, crushed**
2 **cloves garlic, minced**
⅓ **cup pitted Kalamata olives or pitted ripe olives, sliced**
2 **tablespoons snipped fresh Italian (flat-leaf) parsley Black pepper**
4 **cups hot cooked wholegrain penne pasta**
4 **tablespoons grated or shredded Parmesan cheese**

bowls of goodness

A satisfying one-bowl meal brings comfort at the end of a jam-packed day. Put your slow cooker to work on one of these soups, stews, chowders, or chilies that will soothe, satisfy, and delight—without doing in your meal plan.

Coconut-Chicken Curry Stew

15g
CARB PER SERVING

PREP: 20 minutes **SLOW COOK:** 6 to 8 hours (low) or 3 to 4 hours (high)
MAKES: 6 servings (1 cup each)

Nonstick cooking spray
1 cup skinless, boneless chicken thighs cut into 1-inch pieces (about 8 ounces)
6 medium carrots, chopped (3 cups)
2 large onions, coarsely chopped (2 cups)
6 cloves garlic, minced
1 tablespoon grated fresh ginger
1 14.5-ounce can reduced-sodium chicken broth
1 cup light coconut milk
1 tablespoon curry powder
½ teaspoon salt
¼ cup snipped fresh cilantro
1 tablespoon lemon juice

1. Lightly coat an unheated medium nonstick skillet with cooking spray. Heat over medium-high heat; add chicken. Cook and stir about 3 minutes or until lightly browned; drain chicken if necessary.
2. In a 3½- or 4-quart slow cooker layer carrots, chicken, onions, garlic, and ginger. In a medium bowl whisk together broth, coconut milk, curry powder, and salt. Pour over mixture in cooker.
3. Cover and cook on low-heat setting for 6 to 8 hours or on high-heat setting for 3 to 4 hours. To serve, stir in cilantro and lemon juice.

PER SERVING: 174 cal., 5 g total fat (2 g sat. fat), 63 mg chol., 478 mg sodium, 15 g carb. (3 g fiber, 6 g sugars), 17 g pro. Exchanges: 0.5 starch, 2 lean meat, 1 vegetable, 0.5 fat.

Cook Well: Fresh gingerroot from the produce section brings a peppery, slightly sweet flavor to dishes. Look for ginger with smooth, unwrinkled skin. To peel, use a metal spoon to gently scrape away the thin outer coating or use a vegetable peeler. Finely chop the yellow flesh with a sharp chef's knife or grate it with a Microplane or box grater.

Peel and chop ginger as you need it. Wrap unused, unpeeled ginger in plastic wrap and store in the refrigerator up to 2 weeks. Or place in a freezer bag and freeze up to 6 months. Frozen gingerroot is easy to peel and grate.

Soy-Ginger Soup with Chicken

12g CARB PER SERVING

PREP: 20 minutes **SLOW COOK:** 4 to 6 hours (low) or 2 to 3 hours (high), plus 3 minutes
MAKES: 6 servings (1½ cups each)

Nonstick cooking spray
1 pound skinless, boneless chicken thighs, cut into 1-inch pieces
2 medium carrots, coarsely shredded (1 cup)
2 tablespoons dry sherry (optional)
1 tablespoon reduced-sodium soy sauce
1 tablespoon rice vinegar
1 tablespoon grated fresh ginger or 1½ teaspoons ground ginger
¼ teaspoon black pepper
4½ cups water
1 14.5-ounce can reduced-sodium chicken broth
2 ounces dried somen noodles
1 6-ounce package frozen snow pea pods, thawed, or 2 cups fresh snow peas, trimmed
Fresh cilantro sprigs (optional)

1. Lightly coat an unheated large skillet with cooking spray. Brown chicken in hot skillet over medium heat; drain chicken if necessary. Transfer chicken to a 3½- or 4-quart slow cooker; add carrots, sherry (if desired), soy sauce, vinegar, ginger, and pepper. Stir in the water and broth.

2. Cover and cook on low-heat setting for 4 to 6 hours or on high-heat setting for 2 to 3 hours.

3. Break noodles in half. Stir noodles and pea pods into cooker. Cover and cook for 3 minutes more. If desired, garnish each serving with cilantro.

PER SERVING: 152 cal., 3 g total fat (1 g sat. fat), 63 mg chol., 511 mg sodium, 12 g carb. (2 g fiber, 2 g sugars), 18 g pro. Exchanges: 0.5 starch, 2 lean meat, 0.5 vegetable.

Creamy Chicken Noodle Soup

11 g CARB PER SERVING

PREP: 25 minutes **SLOW COOK:** 6 to 8 hours (low) or 3 to 4 hours (high), plus 20 to 30 minutes (high)
MAKES: 8 servings (1½ cups each)

1. In a 5- to 6-quart slow cooker combine broth, the water, chicken, carrots, celery, mushrooms, onion, thyme, and garlic-pepper seasoning.
2. Cover and cook on low-heat setting for 6 to 8 hours or on high-heat setting for 3 to 4 hours.
3. If using low-heat setting, turn to high-heat setting. Stir in cream cheese until combined. Stir in uncooked noodles. Cover and cook for 20 to 30 minutes more or just until noodles are tender.

PER SERVING: 170 cal., 6 g total fat (2 g sat. fat), 54 mg chol., 401 mg sodium, 11 g carb. (2 g fiber, 3 g sugars), 17 g pro. Exchanges: 0.5 starch, 2 lean meat, 0.5 vegetable, 0.5 fat.

- 1 32-ounce container reduced-sodium chicken broth
- 3 cups water
- 2½ cups chopped cooked chicken (about 12 ounces)
- 3 medium carrots, sliced (1½ cups)
- 3 stalks celery, sliced (1½ cups)
- 1½ cups sliced fresh mushrooms (4 ounces)
- ¼ cup chopped onion
- 1½ teaspoons dried thyme, crushed
- ¾ teaspoon garlic-pepper seasoning
- 3 ounces reduced-fat cream cheese (Neufchâtel), cut up
- 2 cups dried egg noodles

Albondigas Soup

12g CARB PER SERVING

PREP: 30 minutes **COOK:** 10 minutes **SLOW COOK:** 8 to 10 hours (low) or 4 to 5 hours (high), plus 30 minutes (high)
MAKES: 8 servings (1⅓ cups soup with 4 meatballs each)

1. In a medium bowl stir together egg, oats, 2 tablespoons onion, 2 tablespoons cilantro, chili powder, oregano, and salt. Gently mix in the ground turkey. Shape meat mixture into 32 (about 1-inch) small meatballs.* In a large nonstick skillet brown meatballs, half at a time, on all sides over medium heat; set aside.
2. In a 4- to 5-quart slow cooker stir together the broth, tomatoes, zucchini, water, ½ cup onion, carrot, garlic, paprika, and chipotle chile powder.
3. Cover and cook on low-heat setting for 8 to 10 hours or on high-heat setting for 4 to 5 hours. If using low-heat setting, turn to high-heat setting. Stir in rice. Cover and cook for 30 minutes more or until rice is tender. Garnish with cilantro.

***Test Kitchen Tip:** If mixture is too soft to work with, scoop the meatballs out using a cookie scoop and arrange on a waxed paper-lined baking sheet. Cover and chill about 30 minutes. Roll into balls as directed.

PER SERVING: 129 cal., 2 g total fat (1 g sat. fat), 51 mg chol., 443 mg sodium, 12 g carb. (2 g fiber, 4 g sugars), 17 g pro. Exchanges: 1 starch, 2 lean meat.

1 egg, lightly beaten
3 tablespoons quick-cooking rolled oats
2 tablespoons finely chopped onion
2 tablespoons snipped fresh cilantro
1 teaspoon chili powder
1 teaspoon dried oregano, crushed
¼ teaspoon salt
1 pound ground turkey breast
4 cups reduced-sodium chicken broth
1 14.5-ounce can no-salt-added diced tomatoes, undrained
1 medium zucchini, sliced (1¼ cups)
1 cup water
1 medium onion, chopped (½ cup)
1 medium carrot, chopped (½ cup)
2 cloves garlic, minced
1 teaspoon smoked paprika
¼ to ½ teaspoon chipotle chile powder
½ cup quick-cooking brown rice
Fresh cilantro

Moroccan-Spiced Chicken Lentil Stew

26g CARB PER SERVING

PREP: 30 minutes **SLOW COOK:** 7 to 8 hours (low) or 3½ to 4 hours (high), plus 15 minutes (high)
MAKES: 8 servings (1⅓ cups each)

2 **pounds skinless, boneless chicken thighs, fat trimmed and cut into 2- to 3-inch chunks**
2 **cloves garlic, minced**
½ **teaspoon ground cumin**
½ **teaspoon ground coriander**
¼ **teaspoon black pepper**
¼ **teaspoon ground cinnamon**
  Nonstick cooking spray
1¼ **cups dry brown lentils, rinsed and drained**
1 **medium onion, cut into thin wedges**
2 **14.5-ounce cans reduced-sodium chicken broth**
1 **cup water**
1 **large yellow summer squash, quartered lengthwise and cut into 1-inch-thick pieces**
½ **cup snipped dried apricots or golden raisins**
2 **tablespoons sliced green onion (1) (optional)**

1. In a large bowl combine chicken, garlic, cumin, coriander, pepper, and cinnamon; toss to coat. Lightly coat an unheated extra-large nonstick skillet with cooking spray. Heat over medium heat; add chicken. Cook until browned, turning to brown all sides.
2. Transfer chicken to a 4- to 5-quart slow cooker. Add lentils and onion to cooker. Pour broth and the water over all in cooker.
3. Cover and cook on low-heat setting for 7 to 8 hours or on high-heat setting for 3½ to 4 hours.
4. If using low-heat setting, turn to high-heat setting. Add squash and apricots to slow cooker. Cover and cook about 15 minutes more or just until squash is tender. If desired, sprinkle each serving with green onion.

PER SERVING: 274 cal., 5 g total fat (1 g sat. fat), 94 mg chol., 318 mg sodium, 26 g carb. (10 g fiber, 6 g sugars), 32 g pro. Exchanges: 1 starch, 0.5 fruit, 4 lean meat.

Chicken Chili

23g CARB PER SERVING

PREP: 25 minutes **SLOW COOK:** 5 to 6 hours (low) or 2½ to 3 hours (high)
MAKES: 3 servings (1 cup each)

Nonstick cooking spray
8 ounces skinless, boneless chicken breast halves, cut into 1-inch pieces
1 15-ounce can white kidney beans (cannellini beans) or great northern beans, rinsed and drained
¾ cup reduced-sodium chicken broth
½ cup water
¼ cup chopped onion
⅓ cup chopped green sweet pepper
½ of a small fresh jalapeño chile pepper, seeded and finely chopped*
¼ teaspoon ground cumin
¼ teaspoon dried oregano, crushed
⅛ teaspoon ground white pepper
1 clove garlic, minced
2 tablespoons chopped tomato
2 tablespoons sliced green onion (1)
2 tablespoons shredded reduced-fat Monterey Jack cheese (½ ounce)

1. Lightly coat an unheated medium skillet with cooking spray. Heat skillet over medium-high heat. Brown chicken in hot skillet; drain chicken if necessary.
2. In a 1½-quart slow cooker combine chicken, beans, broth, the water, onion, sweet pepper, chile pepper, cumin, oregano, white pepper, and garlic.
3. Cover and cook on low-heat setting for 5 to 6 hours or on high-heat setting for 2½ to 3 hours. If no heat setting is available, cook for 4 to 5 hours. Sprinkle each serving with tomato, green onion, and cheese.

*Test Kitchen Tip: Because chile peppers contain volatile oils that can burn your skin and eyes, avoid direct contact with them as much as possible. When working with chile peppers, wear plastic or rubber gloves. If your bare hands do touch the peppers, wash your hands and nails well with soap and warm water.

PER SERVING: 194 cal., 2 g total fat (1 g sat. fat), 47 mg chol., 446 mg sodium, 23 g carb. (7 g fiber, 2 g sugars), 28 g pro. Exchanges: 1.5 starch, 2.5 lean meat.

Turkey and Herb Dumpling Soup

29g CARB PER SERVING

PREP: 40 minutes **SLOW COOK:** 6 to 8 hours (low) or 3 to 4 hours (high), plus 30 to 40 minutes (high)
MAKES: 6 servings (1⅔ cups each)

1. In a 4- to 5-quart slow cooker combine onion, celery, and carrots. Place turkey on vegetables. Add broth, water, and pepper to cooker.
2. Cover and cook on low-heat setting for 6 to 8 hours or on high-heat setting for 3 to 4 hours.
3. If using low-heat setting, turn to high-heat setting while preparing the dumplings. For dumplings, in a large bowl combine flour, parsley, sage, thyme, margarine, milk, and egg. Stir just until moistened. Turn dough out onto a lightly floured surface and knead just until dough is smooth.
4. On a lightly floured surface, roll dough into a 10×8-inch rectangle about ¼ inch thick. Using a pizza cutter, cut the dough into 1-inch-wide strips; cut the strips into 1-inch squares. Set aside.
5. Remove turkey from slow cooker. Using two forks, shred the turkey into large pieces. Return turkey to cooker. Slowly add the dumplings, a few at a time, stirring so they won't stick together. Cover and cook on high-heat setting for 30 to 40 minutes more or until dumplings are cooked but tender. The liquid in the slow cooker will thicken as the dumplings cook. Carefully spoon soup into shallow dishes.

*Test Kitchen Tip: If you don't have leftover roasted turkey breast, substitute 1 pound skinless, boneless chicken thighs that have been browned in a nonstick skillet coated with nonstick cooking spray.

PER SERVING: 308 cal., 8 g total fat (2 g sat. fat), 98 mg chol., 585 mg sodium, 29 g carb. (2 g fiber, 3 g sugars), 29 g pro. Exchanges: 1.5 starch, 3 lean meat, 1 vegetable, 1 fat.

1 large onion, chopped (1 cup)
2 stalks celery, chopped (1 cup)
2 carrots, chopped (1 cup)
1 1-pound piece roasted skinless, boneless turkey breast*
3 cups no-salt-added chicken stock or broth
3 cups water
¼ teaspoon black pepper
1½ cups self-rising flour
1 tablespoon chopped fresh parsley
1 tablespoon chopped fresh sage or 1 teaspoon dried sage, crushed
1 tablespoon chopped fresh thyme or 1 teaspoon dried thyme, crushed
3 tablespoons margarine, melted
3 tablespoons fat-free milk
1 egg, beaten

Turkey Tortellini Soup

25g CARB PER SERVING

PREP: 25 minutes **SLOW COOK:** 6 to 8 hours (low) or 3 to 4 hours (high), plus 30 minutes (high)
MAKES: 6 servings (2 cups each)

1. In a 5- to 6-quart slow cooker combine broth, the water, chopped turkey, tomatoes, and Italian seasoning.
2. Cover and cook on low-heat setting for 6 to 8 hours or on high-heat setting for 3 to 4 hours. If using low-heat setting, turn to high-heat setting. Stir in tortellini. Cover and cook for 30 minutes more or until tortellini is tender. Stir in spinach. If desired, sprinkle each serving with 1 tablespoon cheese.

PER SERVING: 240 cal., 3 g total fat (2 g sat. fat), 63 mg chol., 656 mg sodium, 25 g carb. (3 g fiber, 4 g sugars), 28 g pro. Exchanges: 1 starch, 1 lean meat, 1 vegetable.

- 4 cups reduced-sodium chicken broth
- 4 cups water
- 4 cups coarsely chopped roasted turkey breast (1 pound)
- 1 14.5-ounce can no-salt-added diced tomatoes, undrained
- 1 tablespoon dried Italian seasoning, crushed
- 1 9-ounce package refrigerated cheese tortellini
- 2 cups fresh baby spinach
- 6 tablespoons shredded Parmesan cheese (optional)

Dijon Beef Stew

PREP: 25 minutes   **SLOW COOK:** 8 to 10 hours (low) or 4 to 5 hours (high)
MAKES: 6 servings (1¼ cups each)

2 **cups frozen small whole onions**

2 **cups packaged peeled fresh baby carrots**

1 **pound beef stew meat, trimmed of fat**

1 **14.5-ounce can no-salt-added diced tomatoes, undrained**

1 **14.5-ounce can lower-sodium beef broth**

2 **tablespoons Dijon-style mustard**

4 **cloves garlic, minced**

1 **teaspoon dried thyme, crushed**

½ **teaspoon dried tarragon, crushed**

¼ **teaspoon black pepper**

2 **tablespoons snipped fresh parsley or tarragon**

1. Place onions and carrots in a 3½- or 4-quart slow cooker. Top with stew meat. In a small bowl stir together the tomatoes, broth, mustard, garlic, thyme, tarragon, and pepper. Pour over beef in cooker.
2. Cover and cook on low-heat setting for 8 to 10 hours or on high-heat setting for 4 to 5 hours. Ladle into bowls and sprinkle each serving with parsley.

PER SERVING: 164 cal., 4 g total fat (2 g sat. fat), 48 mg chol., 370 mg sodium, 14 g carb. (4 g fiber, 7 g sugars), 19 g pro. Exchanges: 0.5 starch, 2.5 lean meat, 1 vegetable.

Time-Saving Trick: Purchase lean stew meat if your supermarket offers it. You may pay a bit more per pound, but you won't have to spend much time trimming fat.

Lentil Soup with Beef and Red Pepper

24g
CARB PER SERVING

PREP: 25 minutes **SLOW COOK:** 7 to 8 hours (low) or 3½ to 4 hours (high)
MAKES: 6 servings (1⅓ cups each)

1 **pound boneless beef sirloin steak**
4 **cups lower-sodium beef broth**
1 **cup dry French lentils, rinsed and drained**
1 **cup water**
1 **medium red sweet pepper, coarsely chopped (¾ cup)**
1 **medium onion, chopped (½ cup)**
1 **medium carrot, sliced (½ cup)**
1 **stalk celery, sliced (½ cup)**
2 **cloves garlic, minced**
1 **teaspoon ground cumin**
¼ **teaspoon cayenne pepper**
⅓ **cup snipped fresh parsley**

1. Trim fat from beef. Cut beef into ¾-inch pieces. If desired, in a nonstick skillet cook beef over medium-high heat until browned on all sides. Place beef in a 3½- or 4-quart slow cooker. Stir in broth, lentils, water, sweet pepper, onion, carrot, celery, garlic, cumin, and cayenne pepper.

2. Cover and cook on low-heat setting for 7 to 8 hours or on high-heat setting for 3½ to 4 hours. Stir in parsley.

PER SERVING: 265 cal., 7 g total fat (2 g sat. fat), 50 mg chol., 353 mg sodium, 24 g carb. (11 g fiber, 3 g sugars), 26 g pro. Exchanges: 1 starch, 3 lean meat, 0.5 vegetable.

Southwestern Steak and Potato Soup

12 g
CARB PER SERVING

PREP: 30 minutes **SLOW COOK:** 8 to 10 hours (low) or 4 to 5 hours (high)
MAKES: 14 servings (1 cup each)

1. Trim fat from beef. Cut beef into ¾-inch pieces. Set aside.
2. In a 6-quart slow cooker combine potatoes, green beans, and onion. Add beef. Sprinkle with basil and garlic. Pour salsa and broth over meat and vegetable mixture in cooker.
3. Cover and cook on low-heat setting for 8 to 10 hours or on high-heat setting for 4 to 5 hours. Stir before serving.

PER SERVING: 142 cal., 3 g total fat (1 g sat. fat), 27 mg chol., 532 mg sodium, 12 g carb. (3 g fiber, 3 g sugars), 17 g pro. Exchanges: 1 starch, 2 lean meat.

- 2 **pounds boneless beef sirloin steak, cut ¾ inch thick**
- 3 **medium potatoes, cut into ¾-inch pieces (3 cups)**
- 1 **16-ounce package frozen cut green beans**
- 1 **medium onion, sliced and separated into rings**
- 2 **teaspoons dried basil, crushed**
- 4 **cloves garlic, minced**
- 2 **16-ounce jars thick and chunky salsa**
- 2 **14.5-ounce cans lower-sodium beef broth**

Beef-Vegetable Soup

PREP: 25 minutes **SLOW COOK:** 8 to 10 hours (low) or 4 to 5 hours (high)
MAKES: 4 servings (2 cups each)

1 **pound boneless beef chuck roast, cut into 1-inch pieces**
1 **tablespoon vegetable oil**
2 **14.5-ounce cans no-salt-added diced tomatoes, undrained**
1 **cup water**
3 **medium carrots, sliced (1½ cups)**
2 **small potatoes, peeled (if desired) and cut into ½-inch cubes**
1 **large onion, chopped (1 cup) or 1 cup halved boiling onions**
½ **teaspoon salt**
½ **teaspoon dried thyme, crushed**
½ **cup frozen peas, thawed Fresh Italian (flat-leaf) parsley sprigs**

1. In a large skillet brown meat in hot oil over medium-high heat. Transfer meat to a 3½- to 4½-quart slow cooker. Add tomatoes, the water, carrots, potatoes, onion, salt, and thyme to cooker.
2. Cover and cook on low-heat setting for 8 to 10 hours or on high-heat setting for 4 or 5 hours. Stir in peas. Garnish each serving with parsley.

PER SERVING: 314 cal., 8 g total fat (2 g sat. fat), 50 mg chol., 517 mg sodium, 30 g carb. (7 g fiber, 12 g sugars), 30 g pro. Exchanges: 1 starch, 3.5 lean meat, 2 vegetable, 0.5 fat.

Stuffed Pepper Soup

22g
CARB PER SERVING

PREP: 25 minutes **SLOW COOK:** 8 to 10 hours (low) or 4 to 5 hours (high), plus 30 minutes (high)
MAKES: 8 servings (1¼ cups each)

1. In a large skillet cook beef, onion, sweet peppers, and garlic over medium heat until meat is browned and vegetables are tender. Drain off fat.
2. In a 4- to 5-quart slow cooker combine beef-vegetable mixture, broth, the water, tomatoes, black pepper, chili powder, and smoked paprika.
3. Cover and cook on low-heat setting for 8 to 10 hours or on high-heat setting for 4 to 5 hours. If using low-heat setting, turn to high-heat setting. Stir in rice. Cover and cook for 30 minutes more or until heated through. Sprinkle each serving with cheese.

PER SERVING: 218 cal., 7 g total fat (3 g sat. fat), 37 mg chol., 405 mg sodium, 22 g carb. (2 g fiber, 4 g sugars), 17 g pro. Exchanges: 1 starch, 2 lean meat, 1 vegetable, 0.5 fat.

1 pound lean ground beef
1 large onion, chopped (1 cup)
1 medium red sweet pepper, chopped (½ cup)
1 medium orange sweet pepper, chopped (½ cup)
1 medium green sweet pepper, chopped (½ cup)
2 cloves garlic, minced
4 cups lower-sodium beef broth
2 cups water
1 14.5-ounce can diced tomatoes, undrained
½ teaspoon black pepper
½ teaspoon chili powder
½ teaspoon smoked paprika
¾ cup uncooked instant brown rice
½ cup finely shredded Colby and Monterey Jack cheese (2 ounces)

Caribbean Pork Chili

32g CARB PER SERVING

PREP: 20 minutes **SLOW COOK:** 4 to 5 hours (low) or 2 to 2½ hours (high)
MAKES: 6 servings (1½ cups each)

1½ pounds boneless pork loin roast, cut into 1-inch pieces
1 tablespoon chili powder
2 cloves garlic, minced
½ teaspoon ground chipotle chile pepper (optional)
½ teaspoon ground cumin
¼ teaspoon salt
1 tablespoon canola oil
2 14.5-ounce cans no-salt-added diced tomatoes, undrained
1 15-ounce can no-salt-added black beans, rinsed and drained
1 8-ounce can no-salt-added tomato sauce
1 cup frozen whole kernel corn
1 medium mango, halved, seeded, peeled, and chopped
¼ cup snipped fresh cilantro
¼ cup red onion shards (optional)

1. In a medium bowl combine pork, chili powder, garlic, ground chile pepper (if using), cumin, and salt; toss to coat.
2. In a large nonstick skillet heat oil over medium-high heat. Cook pork, half at a time, in hot skillet until browned on all sides, stirring occasionally. Transfer pork to a 3½- or 4-quart slow cooker. Add tomatoes, beans, tomato sauce, and frozen corn to cooker.
3. Cover and cook on low-heat setting for 4 to 5 hours or on high-heat setting for 2 to 2½ hours. Combine mango, cilantro, and, if desired, onion shards. Spoon mixture over top of each serving.

PER SERVING: 315 cal., 7 g total fat (2 g sat. fat), 78 mg chol., 246 mg sodium, 32 g carb. (8 g fiber, 12 g sugars), 32 g pro. Exchanges: 2 starch, 3.5 lean meat, 1 vegetable.

Cook Well: Most canned beans can be used interchangeably in chili recipes. Try one of these beans:
- **Pinto:** These small beans are pinkish brown and rich in flavor.
- **Kidney:** These classic chili beans have dark to light red skin, creamy flesh, and full-bodied flavor.
- **Garbanzo:** Also called chickpeas, these beans have a nutlike flavor and firm texture.
- **Navy:** Sometimes called Yankee beans, these are small and white.
- **Great Northern:** These white beans are slightly grainy and have a delicate flavor.
- **Cannellini:** This white Italian kidney bean has a creamy texture.

Pork and Black Bean Soup

24g CARB PER SERVING

PREP: 25 minutes **STAND:** 1 hour **SLOW COOK:** 8 to 10 hours (low) or 4 to 5 hours (high)
MAKES: 6 servings (1¼ cups each)

1 cup dry black beans, rinsed and drained
6 cups water
1 pound boneless pork loin
4 cups reduced-sodium chicken broth
1 cup water
1 medium onion, chopped (½ cup)
1 medium carrot, chopped (½ cup)
1 small green sweet pepper, chopped (½ cup)
½ cup bottled chipotle salsa or salsa
1 teaspoon ground cumin
½ teaspoon liquid smoke
1 clove garlic, minced
Snipped fresh cilantro

1. In a large pot combine beans and the 6 cups water. Bring to boiling; reduce heat. Simmer, uncovered, for 10 minutes. Remove from heat. Cover and let stand for 1 hour. Drain and rinse beans. Meanwhile, trim fat from pork. Cut pork into ¾-inch pieces.
2. In a 3½- or 4-quart slow cooker combine drained beans, pork, broth, 1 cup water, onion, carrot, sweet pepper, salsa, cumin, liquid smoke, and garlic.
3. Cover and cook on low-heat setting for 8 to 10 hours or on high-heat setting for 4 to 5 hours. Sprinkle each serving with cilantro.

PER SERVING: 259 cal., 7 g total fat (2 g sat. fat), 52 mg chol., 513 mg sodium, 24 g carb. (6 g fiber, 3 g sugars), 24 g pro. Exchanges: 1.5 starch, 3 lean meat, 0.5 vegetable.

Pork Zuppa

(19 g CARB PER SERVING)

PREP: 30 minutes **SLOW COOK:** 6 to 8 hours (low) or 3 to 4 hours (high), plus 30 to 60 minutes (high)
MAKES: 6 servings (1⅓ cups each)

1. In a large skillet cook pork, onion, and garlic over medium heat until meat is browned and onion is tender; drain off fat. Return meat mixture to skillet; add oregano, salt, and crushed red pepper. Cook for 1 minute more. Transfer to a 3½- or 4-quart slow cooker. Add broth and potatoes.
2. Cover and cook on low-heat setting for 6 to 8 hours or on high-heat setting for 3 to 4 hours. If using low-heat setting, turn to high-heat setting. In a small bowl combine evaporated milk and cornstarch until smooth; stir into cooker. Stir in kale. Cover and cook for 30 to 60 minutes more or until bubbly around edges of cooker. If desired, sprinkle with additional crushed red pepper.

PER SERVING: 303 cal., 12 g total fat (4 g sat. fat), 53 mg chol., 542 mg sodium, 19 g carb. (2 g fiber, 4 g sugars), 20 g pro. Exchanges: 1 starch, 2 medium-fat meat, 1 vegetable, 1 fat.

- 1 **pound ground pork**
- 1 **large onion, chopped (1 cup)**
- 2 **cloves garlic, minced**
- 1 **teaspoon dried oregano, crushed**
- ¼ **teaspoon salt**
- ¼ **to ½ teaspoon crushed red pepper**
- 4 **cups reduced-sodium chicken broth**
- 12 **ounces tiny red new potatoes, each cut into 8 pieces**
- 1 **12-ounce can fat-free evaporated milk**
- 2 **tablespoons cornstarch**
- 2 **cups chopped fresh kale Crushed red pepper (optional)**

Creamy Ham and Potato Chowder

27g
CARB PER
SERVING

PREP: 20 minutes **SLOW COOK:** 3 hours (high), plus 30 minutes (high)
MAKES: 6 servings (1⅓ cups each)

12 **ounces tiny yellow potatoes, cut into ¾-inch pieces**

1 **large onion, chopped (1 cup)**

2 **14.5-ounce cans reduced-sodium chicken broth**

¼ **cup cornstarch**

½ **teaspoon dried thyme, crushed**

¼ **teaspoon black pepper**

1 **12-ounce can (1½ cups) evaporated fat-free milk**

½ **cup diced cooked lean ham**

2 **medium carrots, coarsely shredded (1 cup)**

1 **cup broccoli florets, steamed**

¼ **cup shredded cheddar cheese (1 ounce)**

2 **teaspoons snipped fresh thyme (optional)**

1. In a 4-quart slow cooker combine potatoes and onion. Pour broth over vegetables.
2. Cover and cook on high-heat setting for 3 hours.
3. In a medium bowl combine cornstarch, dried thyme, and pepper. Whisk in evaporated milk. Stir the cornstarch mixture, ham, and carrots into the cooker. Cover and cook for 30 minutes more, stirring the soup occasionally. Serve soup topped with broccoli and cheese. If desired, sprinkle with fresh thyme.

PER SERVING: 171 cal., 2 g total fat (1 g sat. fat), 12 mg chol., 566 mg sodium, 27 g carb. (3 g fiber, 10 g sugars), 11 g pro. Exchanges: 1 starch, 0.5 milk, 0.5 lean meat, 0.5 vegetable.

Clam Chowder

27 g CARB PER SERVING

PREP: 35 minutes **SLOW COOK:** 7 hours (low) or 3½ hours (high), plus 30 to 60 minutes (high)
MAKES: 6 servings (1⅓ cups each)

1. In a 3½- or 4-quart slow cooker combine celery, onions, potatoes, carrots, the water, clam juice, broth, thyme, pepper, and bay leaf.
2. Cover and cook on low-heat setting for 7 hours or on high-heat setting for 3½ hours.
3. If using low-heat setting, turn to high-heat setting. In a medium bowl combine evaporated milk and cornstarch. Stir milk mixture, clams, and sherry (if desired) into cooker. Cover and cook for 30 to 60 minutes more or until bubbly around edge. Stir in vinegar just before serving. Remove bay leaf and discard. stir in bacon and, if desired, parsley.

PER SERVING: 222 cal., 2 g total fat (1 g sat. fat), 48 mg chol., 599 mg sodium, 27 g carb. (3 g fiber, 10 g sugars), 25 g pro. Exchanges: 1.5 starch, 3 lean meat, 0.5 vegetable.

Time-Saving Trick: Chopping fresh vegetables by hand takes only a few minutes. However, you can save time with the help of a food processor. Use on-off pulses to help control the size of the chopped vegetables.

3 stalks celery, chopped (1½ cups)
3 medium onions, chopped (1½ cups)
1½ cups chopped red-skin potatoes
2 medium carrots, chopped (1 cup)
1¼ cups water
1 8-ounce bottle clam juice
1 cup reduced-sodium chicken broth or low-sodium vegetable broth
1½ teaspoons dried thyme, crushed
½ teaspoon coarsely ground black pepper
1 bay leaf
1 12-ounce can fat-free evaporated milk
3 tablespoons cornstarch
2 6.5-ounce cans chopped clams, drained
2 tablespoons dry sherry (optional)
1 teaspoon red wine vinegar
2 slices turkey bacon, cooked according to package directions and chopped Snipped fresh parsley (optional)

Hot-and-Sour Soup

11 g CARB PER SERVING

PREP: 20 minutes **SLOW COOK:** 6 to 8 hours (low) or 3 to 4 hours (high), plus 10 to 15 minutes (high)
MAKES: 6 servings (1¼ cups each)

2 14.5-ounce cans reduced-sodium chicken broth
2 medium carrots, bias-sliced (1 cup)
1 8-ounce can bamboo shoots, drained
1 8-ounce can sliced water chestnuts, drained
½ cup water
1 4-ounce can (drained weight) sliced mushrooms, drained
3 tablespoons rice vinegar or white vinegar
1 tablespoon reduced-sodium soy sauce
1 teaspoon sugar*
¼ teaspoon crushed red pepper
2 tablespoons cornstarch
2 tablespoons cold water
8 ounces frozen peeled and deveined uncooked shrimp, thawed**
4 ounces refrigerated water-packed firm tofu (fresh bean curd), drained and cubed
2 tablespoons snipped fresh parsley or cilantro (optional)

1. In a 3½- or 4-quart slow cooker combine broth, carrots, bamboo shoots, water chestnuts, the ½ cup water, the mushrooms, vinegar, soy sauce, sugar (if using), and crushed red pepper.
2. Cover and cook on low-heat setting for 6 to 8 hours or on high-heat setting for 3 to 4 hours.
3. If using low-heat setting, turn to high-heat setting. In a small bowl stir together cornstarch and the 2 tablespoons cold water; stir into chicken broth mixture in slow cooker. Add shrimp and the tofu. Cover and cook for 10 to 15 minutes more. Stir in sugar substitute (if using). Sprinkle each serving with parsley.

*Sugar Substitutes: Choose from Splenda Granular or Sweet'N Low bulk or packets. Follow package directions to use product amount equivalent to 1 teaspoon sugar. Stir in sugar substitute after cooking.

**Test Kitchen Tip: If desired, leave tails on shrimp.

PER SERVING: 98 cal., 1 g total fat (0 g sat. fat), 48 mg chol., 739 mg sodium, 11 g carb. (2 g fiber, 3 g sugars), 9 g pro. Exchanges: 0.5 starch, 1 lean meat, 0.5 vegetable.

PER SERVING WITH SUBSTITUTE: Same as above, except 96 cal.

On the Side: Put this soup on to simmer in the morning. Before you leave work that night, order some vegetarian nonfried spring rolls from an Asian restaurant to pick up on your way home.

Vegetarian Black Bean Soup

37 g
CARB PER SERVING

PREP: 10 minutes **STAND:** 1 hour **SLOW COOK:** 9 to 10 hours (low) or 4½ to 5 hours (high)
MAKES: 6 servings (1⅓ cups each)

1. In a large pot combine beans and the 8 cups water. Bring to boiling; reduce heat. Simmer, uncovered, for 10 minutes. Remove from heat. Cover and let stand for 1 hour. Drain and rinse beans.
2. In a 4-quart slow cooker combine drained beans, onion, jalapeño, garlic, broth, cumin, chili powder, and salt.
3. Cover and cook on low-heat setting for 9 to 10 hours or on high-heat setting for 4½ to 5 hours. Use a potato masher to coarsely mash the beans. Top each serving with cilantro and serve with lime slices or wedges for squeezing. If desired, top each serving with sour cream.

*Test Kitchen Tip: Because chile peppers contain volatile oils that can burn your skin and eyes, avoid direct contact with them as much as possible. When working with chile peppers, wear plastic or rubber gloves. If your bare hands do touch the peppers, wash your hands and nails well with soap and warm water.

PER SERVING: 204 cal., 1 g total fat (0 g sat. fat), 0 mg chol., 367 mg sodium, 37 g carb. (10 g fiber, 4 g sugars), 11 g pro. Exchanges: 2.5 starch, 0.5 lean meat.

10 ounces dry black beans (1½ cups), rinsed and drained
 8 cups water
 1 medium onion, chopped (½ cup)
 1 fresh jalapeño chile pepper, seeded and chopped*
 3 cloves garlic, minced
 6 cups no-salt-added vegetable broth
 2 tablespoons ground cumin
 1 tablespoon chili powder
 ½ teaspoon salt
 ½ cup chopped fresh cilantro or cilantro sprigs
     Lime slices or wedges
     Light sour cream (optional)

Vegetable and Bean Soup

PREP: 25 minutes **SLOW COOK:** 6 to 8 hours (low) or 3 to 4 hours (high), plus 1 hour (high)
MAKES: 8 servings (1¼ cups each)

1 **32-ounce carton reduced-sodium chicken broth**
1 **23.5-ounce jar lower-sodium Italian pasta sauce**
1 **pint cherry or grape tomatoes, halved**
2 **cups fresh green beans, cut into 1-inch pieces**
1 **15-ounce can no-salt-added cannellini beans (white kidney beans), rinsed and drained**
1 **cup chopped fresh mushrooms**
2 **medium carrots, sliced (1 cup)**
1 **medium yellow sweet pepper, chopped (¾ cup)**
1 **medium onion, chopped (½ cup)**
¼ **cup finely chopped ham**
1 **teaspoon dried Italian seasoning, crushed**
2 **cloves garlic, minced**
¼ **teaspoon black pepper**
2 **cups chopped fresh cabbage**
½ **cup dried tiny pasta, such as orzo or ditalini**

1. In a 5- to 6-quart slow cooker combine broth, pasta sauce, tomatoes, green beans, cannellini beans, mushrooms, carrots, sweet pepper, onion, ham, Italian seasoning, garlic, and black pepper. Stir gently to mix.

2. Cover and cook on low-heat setting for 6 to 8 hours or on high-heat setting for 3 to 4 hours. If using low-heat setting, turn to high-heat setting. Stir in cabbage and pasta. Cover and cook for 1 hour more or until pasta is tender.

PER SERVING: 183 cal., 4 g total fat (1 g sat. fat), 2 mg chol., 569 mg sodium, 29 g carb. (6 g fiber, 10 g sugars), 8 g pro. Exchanges: 1.5 starch, 1 vegetable, 0.5 fat.

Savory Bean and Spinach Soup

31g CARB PER SERVING

PREP: 15 minutes **SLOW COOK:** 5 to 7 hours (low) or 2½ to 3½ hours (high)
MAKES: 6 servings (1½ cups each)

1. In a 3½- or 4-quart slow cooker combine the water, tomato puree, beans, broth, onions, rice, basil, pepper, and garlic.
2. Cover and cook on low-heat setting for 5 to 7 hours or on high-heat setting for 2½ to 3½ hours.
3. Before serving, stir in spinach. Sprinkle each serving with Parmesan cheese.

PER SERVING: 148 cal., 1 g total fat (0 g sat. fat), 1 mg chol., 451 mg sodium, 31 g carb. (5 g fiber, 3 g sugars), 8 g pro. Exchanges: 1.5 starch, 1.5 vegetable.

3½ cups water
1 15-ounce can tomato puree
1 15-ounce can small white beans or Great Northern beans, rinsed and drained
1 14.5-ounce can vegetable broth
2 small onions, finely chopped (⅔ cup)
½ cup uncooked converted rice
1½ teaspoons dried basil, crushed
¼ teaspoon black pepper
2 cloves garlic, minced
8 cups coarsely chopped fresh spinach
2 tablespoons finely shredded Parmesan cheese

so-good sandwiches

Dish up some hot and saucy fillings from your slow cooker to spoon into breads, buns, pitas, or tortillas for health-smart sandwiches that are as much at home at festive gatherings as at casual weeknight meals.

Cuban Sandwiches

25g CARB PER SERVING

PREP: 30 minutes **SLOW COOK:** 8 to 9 hours (low) or 4 to 4½ hours (high), plus 30 minutes (high)
MAKES: 10 servings (1 open-face sandwich each)

1 2½- to 3-pound pork sirloin roast
1 teaspoon dry mustard
½ teaspoon ground cumin
½ teaspoon black pepper
½ cup water
1 recipe Dilled Cucumbers
3 medium sweet peppers, thinly sliced crosswise
2 medium banana peppers, seeded and sliced crosswise
2 tablespoons yellow mustard
5 whole grain ciabatta buns, split (about 12 ounces total)
4 ounces thinly sliced cooked lower-sodium ham

1. Trim fat from roast. If necessary, cut roast to fit in a 3½- or 4-quart slow cooker. Place roast in cooker. In a small bowl combine dry mustard, cumin, and black pepper. Sprinkle over roast. Add the water to cooker.
2. Cover and cook on low-heat setting for 8 to 9 hours or on high-heat setting for 4 to 4½ hours. Meanwhile, prepare Dilled Cucumbers. If using low-heat setting, turn to high-heat setting. Add sweet peppers and banana peppers to slow cooker. Cover and cook on high-heat setting for 30 minutes more.
3. Remove pork from cooker. Using two forks, coarsely shred pork. Stir pork into the cooking liquid in cooker.
4. Spread yellow mustard over split sides of ciabatta buns. Using a slotted spoon, divide pork among bun halves. Top with ham, peppers, and Dilled Cucumbers. If desired, drizzle some of the cucumber liquid over sandwiches.

Dilled Cucumbers: In a large bowl whisk together ½ cup cider vinegar, ¼ cup light mayonnaise, 4 teaspoons snipped fresh dill or 1 teaspoon dried dill weed, and ¼ teaspoon salt. Thinly slice 2 large English cucumbers; add to mayonnaise mixture with ½ of a red onion, cut into slivers. Toss to coat. Cover and chill for 2 to 4 hours before serving.

PER SERVING: 294 cal., 8 g total fat (2 g sat. fat), 72 mg chol., 498 mg sodium, 25 g carb. (3 g fiber, 4 g sugars), 28 g pro. Exchanges: 1.5 starch, 3 lean meat, 1 vegetable, 0.5 fat.

On the Side: For a fiber-packed side with this and other sandwiches, chill a 15-ounce can of black beans while the pork simmers in the slow cooker. Close to dinnertime, drain the chilled beans, rinse them well under cool running water, and drain again. Toss the beans with ½ cup thawed frozen corn, sliced green onions, and a reduced-fat vinaigrette. Chill until ready to serve.

Asian Pork Sandwiches

27 g CARB PER SERVING

PREP: 25 minutes **SLOW COOK:** 10 to 12 hours (low) or 5 to 6 hours (high)
MAKES: 8 servings (1 sandwich each)

- 1 2½- to 3-pound pork shoulder roast
- 1 cup apple juice or apple cider
- 2 tablespoons reduced-sodium soy sauce
- 2 tablespoons bottled hoisin sauce
- 1½ teaspoons five-spice powder
- 8 whole wheat hamburger buns, split and toasted
- 2 cups shredded Chinese (napa) cabbage
- 2 green onions, thinly sliced

1. Trim fat from roast. If necessary, cut roast to fit in a 3½- or 4-quart slow cooker. Place roast in cooker. In a small bowl combine apple juice, soy sauce, hoisin sauce, and five-spice powder. Pour over roast in cooker.
2. Cover and cook on low-heat setting for 10 to 12 hours or on high-heat setting for 5 to 6 hours.
3. Remove meat from cooker, reserving cooking liquid. Remove meat from bone; discard bone. Using two forks, shred meat; discard fat. Place ½ cup meat (about 3 ounces) on each bun bottom. Top with ¼ cup shredded cabbage; add bun tops. Skim fat from cooking liquid. Serve 3 tablespoons cooking liquid each in individual bowls for dipping; sprinkle liquid with green onions.

PER SERVING: 282 cal., 7 g total fat (2 g sat. fat), 61 mg chol., 478 mg sodium, 27 g carb. (3 g fiber, 8 g sugars), 26 g pro. Exchanges: 2 starch, 3 lean meat.

Cook Well: Pork shoulder is a tough, muscular cut perfectly suited to slow cooking. When simmered for hours, the meat becomes fall-apart tender, ultramoist, and boldly flavorful. It's also a relatively inexpensive cut.

Pork shoulder roast is often cut in larger portions than called for in a recipe. If the cut you buy is large, divide the roast into two pieces, cutting one the size you need for your recipe. Wrap the remaining meat in freezer wrap. Label and freeze for up to 4 months. Thaw in the refrigerator before cooking.

Honey Barbecue Shredded Pork Wraps

24g CARB PER SERVING

PREP: 25 minutes SLOW COOK: 13 to 14 hours (low) or 6½ to 7 hours (high)
MAKES: 12 servings (1 wrap each)

1. Trim fat from roast. If necessary, cut roast to fit in a 4- to 5-quart slow cooker. Place roast in cooker. In a medium bowl stir together ketchup, celery, onion, the water, honey, lemon juice, vinegar, mustard, Worcestershire sauce, and pepper. Pour over roast in cooker.
2. Cover and cook on low-heat setting for 13 to 14 hours or on high-heat setting for 6½ to 7 hours.
3. Remove meat from cooker, reserving sauce. Using two forks, shred meat; discard fat. Place meat in a large bowl.
4. Skim fat from sauce. Add enough of the reserved sauce to moisten meat (about 1 cup). Spoon about ⅔ cup pork on top of each tortilla. Roll up and cut in half to serve.

PER SERVING: 326 cal., 10 g total fat (3 g sat. fat), 73 mg chol., 589 mg sodium, 24 g carb., (10 g fiber, 9 g sugars), 31 g pro. Exchanges: 1.5 starch, 4 lean meat.

- 1 3- to 3½-pound boneless pork shoulder roast
- 1 cup ketchup
- 2 stalks celery, chopped (1 cup)
- 1 large onion, chopped (1 cup)
- ½ cup water
- ⅓ cup honey
- ¼ cup lemon juice
- 3 tablespoons white vinegar
- 2 tablespoons dry mustard
- 2 tablespoons Worcestershire sauce
- ½ teaspoon black pepper
- 12 8-inch whole wheat tortillas

Jerk Pork Wraps with Lime Mayo

26g CARB PER SERVING

PREP: 30 minutes **SLOW COOK:** 8 to 10 hours (low) or 4 to 5 hours (high)
MAKES: 6 servings (1 wrap each)

1 1½- to 2-pound boneless pork shoulder roast
1 tablespoon Jamaican jerk seasoning
¼ teaspoon dried thyme, crushed
1 cup water
1 tablespoon lime juice
6 8-inch flour tortillas
6 lettuce leaves (optional)
1 medium red or green sweet pepper, chopped (½ cup)
1 medium mango, peeled, seeded, and chopped
1 recipe Lime Mayo

1. Trim fat from roast. Sprinkle jerk seasoning evenly over roast; rub in with your fingers. Place roast in a 3½- or 4-quart slow cooker. Sprinkle with thyme. Pour the water over roast in cooker.
2. Cover and cook on low-heat setting for 8 to 10 hours or on high-heat setting for 4 to 5 hours.
3. Remove meat from cooker; discard cooking liquid. Using two forks, shred meat; discard fat. Place meat in a medium bowl. Stir lime juice into meat.
4. If desired, line tortillas with lettuce leaves. Spoon ½ cup meat mixture onto the center of each tortilla. Top with about 1 tablespoon sweet pepper, 2 to 3 tablespoons mango, and about 2 tablespoons Lime Mayo. Fold up bottom of each tortilla; fold in sides. Serve immediately.

Lime Mayo: In a small bowl stir together ½ cup fat-free mayonnaise, ¼ cup finely chopped red onion, ¼ teaspoon finely shredded lime peel, 1 tablespoon lime juice, and 1 clove garlic, minced. Cover and store in refrigerator until ready to serve or for up to 1 week.

PER SERVING: 292 cal., 9 g total fat (3 g sat. fat), 73 mg chol., 526 mg sodium, 26 g carb. (2 g fiber, 8 g sugars), 25 g pro. Exchanges: 2 starch, 2.5 lean meat, 1 fat.

Time-Saving Trick: For a head start on tomorrow's simmered-all-day supper, complete these tasks the night before:
- Chop the vegetables as directed and refrigerate them in separate covered containers.
- Assemble, cover, and chill liquid ingredients or sauces in separate covered containers.
- Measure and combine spices and dried herbs; place in a small, tightly covered container and keep at room temperature until needed.
- Brown ground meat, ground poultry, or ground sausage, making sure it's fully cooked before covering and refrigerating. Do not brown other meats, such as chicken, beef, or pork cubes or roasts; partially cooking meats and refrigerating them for later cooking is unsafe.

Mexican-Style Roast Sandwiches

34g CARB PER SERVING

PREP: 30 minutes **COOK:** 18 minutes **SLOW COOK:** 10 to 12 hours (low) or 5 to 6 hours (high)
MAKES: 10 servings (1 sandwich each)

1	3- to 3½-pound boneless pork shoulder roast
4	cloves garlic, thinly sliced
1½	cups vinegar
1	cup fresh cilantro leaves
1	medium onion, cut into wedges
¼	cup water
1	teaspoon dried oregano, crushed
1	teaspoon ground cumin
¼	teaspoon salt
¼	teaspoon black pepper
2	medium red onions, thinly sliced
1	tablespoon vegetable oil
¼	cup lime juice
10	multigrain ciabatta rolls, split and toasted
	Thinly sliced radishes (optional)
	Fresh cilantro sprigs (optional)
	Lime wedges (optional)

1. Trim fat from roast. Using a sharp knife, make slits on all sides of the roast. Insert garlic slices into slits. Place roast in a 3½- or 4-quart slow cooker.
2. In a blender combine vinegar, cilantro leaves, onion wedges, the water, oregano, cumin, salt, and pepper. Cover and blend until smooth. Pour over roast in cooker.
3. Cover and cook on low-heat setting for 10 to 12 hours or on high-heat setting for 5 to 6 hours.
4. Before serving, in a large skillet cook red onions in hot oil about 15 minutes or until tender. Carefully add lime juice to skillet. Cook and stir for 3 to 5 minutes or until lime juice is evaporated.
5. Meanwhile, using a slotted spoon, remove meat from slow cooker, reserving cooking liquid in cooker. Using two forks, shred meat; discard fat. Transfer shredded meat to a large bowl. Add 1 cup of the cooking liquid, tossing to coat.
6. Spoon about ⅔ cup shredded meat onto each roll bottom. If desired, drizzle with additional cooking liquid. Top each with about 2 tablespoons cooked red onions. If desired, top with radishes and cilantro sprigs. Add roll tops. If desired, serve with lime wedges.

PER SERVING: 378 cal., 10 g total fat (3 g sat. fat), 88 mg chol., 496 mg sodium, 34 g carb. (3 g fiber, 2 g sugars), 32 g pro. Exchanges: 2 starch, 3.5 lean meat, 0.5 vegetable.

Asian Lettuce Cups

6g CARB PER SERVING

PREP: 20 minutes **SLOW COOK:** 8 to 10 hours (low) or 4 to 5 hours (high), plus 15 minutes (high)
MAKES: 12 servings (3 filled lettuce cups each)

1. Trim fat from roast. If necessary, cut roast to fit in a 3½- or 4-quart slow cooker. Place roast in cooker. In a medium bowl combine green onions, vinegar, soy sauce, hoisin sauce, ginger, chili oil, and pepper. Pour over meat in cooker.

2. Cover and cook on low-heat setting for 8 to 10 hours or on high-heat setting for 4 to 5 hours. If using low-heat setting, turn to high-heat setting. In a small bowl combine cornstarch and the cold water. Stir cornstarch mixture into liquid around the meat. Cover and cook about 15 minutes more or until thickened.

3. Remove meat from cooker. Using two forks, shred meat. Place meat in a bowl and stir enough of the cooking liquid (about 1 cup) to make meat mixture the desired consistency. Spoon about 2 tablespoons of the meat mixture onto each lettuce leaf "cup." Top meat with jicama, carrots, and sesame seeds. Serve leaf cups like open-face sandwiches.

PER SERVING: 178 cal., 5 g total fat (1 g sat. fat), 67 mg chol., 311 mg sodium, 6 g carb. (1 g fiber, 2 g sugars), 25 g pro. Exchanges: 3.5 lean meat, 0.5 vegetable.

1	**3-pound boneless beef chuck pot roast**
½	**cup chopped green onions (4)**
¼	**cup rice vinegar**
¼	**cup reduced-sodium soy sauce**
2	**tablespoons hoisin sauce**
1	**tablespoon finely chopped fresh ginger**
½	**teaspoon chili oil**
¼	**teaspoon black pepper**
2	**tablespoons cornstarch**
2	**tablespoons cold water**
36	**Bibb or Boston lettuce leaves**
1½	**cups chopped jicama or celery**
1	**cup coarsely shredded carrots**
1	**tablespoon toasted sesame seeds**

Classic French Dips

39g CARB PER SERVING

PREP: 20 minutes **SLOW COOK:** 9 to 10 hours (low) or 4½ to 5 hours (high)
MAKES: 6 servings (1 sandwich and about ½ cup cooking liquid each)

1. Place onion in a 3½- to 5-quart slow cooker. Trim fat from brisket. If necessary, cut brisket to fit in cooker. Place brisket on top of onion. Sprinkle with garlic, thyme, and pepper. Pour beef broth and Worcestershire sauce over all in cooker.
2. Cover and cook on low-heat setting for 9 to 10 hours for brisket or 8 to 9 hours for bottom round or on high-heat setting for 4½ to 5 hours for brisket or 4 to 4½ hours for bottom round.
3. Remove meat from cooker, reserving cooking liquid in cooker. Thinly slice meat across the grain, removing visible fat as you slice. Using a slotted spoon, remove onion from cooker. Place 3 to 4 ounces sliced brisket on top of each bread bottom. Top each with about ⅓ cup onions. Add bread tops. Skim fat from cooking liquid in cooker. Serve cooking liquid in individual bowls for dipping (about ½ cup per serving).

PER SERVING: 339 cal., 7 g total fat (2 g sat. fat), 45 mg chol., 453 mg sodium, 39 g carb. (9 g fiber, 6 g sugars), 33 g pro. Exchanges: 2.5 starch, 3.5 lean meat.

1 large sweet onion (such as Vidalia, Maui, or Walla Walla), cut into ½-inch-thick slices and separated into rings
1 2- to 2½-pound fresh beef brisket or boneless beef bottom round roast
2 cloves garlic, minced
1 teaspoon dried thyme, marjoram, or oregano, crushed
½ teaspoon black pepper
1 14.5-ounce can lower-sodium beef broth
2 tablespoons Worcestershire sauce
1 16-ounce loaf whole grain baguette-style bread, cut crosswise into 6 pieces and split in half horizontally

Beef Fajitas

20g CARB PER SERVING

PREP: 25 minutes **SLOW COOK:** 7 to 8 hours (low) or 3½ to 4 hours (high)
MAKES: 8 servings (1 fajita each)

1   **large onion, cut into thin wedges**
2   **pounds boneless beef sirloin steak**
1   **teaspoon ground cumin**
1   **teaspoon ground coriander**
½   **teaspoon black pepper**
¼   **teaspoon salt**
2   **medium red and/or green sweet peppers, cut into thin bite-size strips**
¼   **cup lower-sodium beef broth**
8   **7- to 8-inch whole wheat or plain flour tortillas**
1   **cup shredded carrots**
1   **cup coarsely shredded lettuce**
½   **cup bottled salsa (optional)**
⅓   **cup purchased guacamole (optional)**
⅓   **cup light sour cream (optional)**

1. Place onion in a 3½- or 4-quart slow cooker. Trim fat from steak. In a small bowl stir together cumin, coriander, black pepper, and salt. Sprinkle mixture over one side of the steak; rub in with your fingers. Cut steak across grain into thin bite-size strips. Add steak strips to cooker. Top with sweet peppers. Pour broth over all in cooker.

2. Cover and cook on low-heat setting for 7 to 8 hours or on high-heat setting for 3½ to 4 hours.

3. Using a slotted spoon, spoon ½ cup beef-vegetable mixture onto each tortilla. Top each serving with carrots and lettuce. Fold tortillas over filling. If desired, serve with salsa, guacamole, and sour cream.

PER SERVING: 298 cal., 8 g total fat (2 g sat. fat), 68 mg chol., 485 mg sodium, 20 g carb. (12 g fiber, 4 g sugars), 33 g pro. Exchanges: 1 starch, 4 lean meat, 0.5 vegetable.

Beef and Vegetable Sandwiches

28g CARB PER SERVING

PREP: 20 minutes **SLOW COOK:** 4 hours (low) or 2 hours (high)
MAKES: 8 servings (1 sandwich each)

1 **pound extra-lean ground beef**
1 **cup frozen mixed vegetables**
1 **cup diced green sweet pepper**
⅓ **cup no-salt-added tomato paste (½ of a 6-ounce can)**
2 **tablespoons balsamic vinegar**
2 **teaspoons Worcestershire sauce**
¾ **teaspoon salt**
8 **reduced-calorie whole grain hamburger buns**

1. In a large nonstick skillet cook ground beef until meat is browned. In a 1½-quart slow cooker combine cooked beef, frozen vegetables, sweet pepper, tomato paste, balsamic vinegar, Worcestershire sauce, and salt.

2. Cover and cook on low-heat setting for 4 hours or on high-heat setting for 2 hours. To serve, spoon about ½ cup beef mixture onto each bun bottom. Add bun tops.

PER SERVING: 226 cal., 5 g total fat (2 g sat. fat), 35 mg chol., 510 mg sodium, 28 g carb. (1 g fiber, 2 g sugars), 17 g pro. Exchanges: 2 starch, 1.5 lean meat.

Open-Face Shredded Beef Sandwiches

PREP: 25 minutes **SLOW COOK:** 9 to 10 hours (low) or 4½ to 5 hours (high)
MAKES: 6 servings (1 open-face sandwich each)

1. Press coffee powder into sides of roast. Coat an unheated medium nonstick skillet with cooking spray; heat over medium-high heat. Add roast; cook until lightly browned turning once.
2. Coat an unheated 3- or 3½-quart slow cooker with cooking spray. Layer onions, pepper, garlic, and bay leaves in cooker. If necessary, cut roast to fit. Place roast on top of vegetables.
3. Add wine to skillet; bring to boiling over medium-high heat, scraping browned bits from bottom and sides of skillet. Remove from heat; stir in vinegar and Worcestershire sauce. Pour over roast.
4. Cover and cook on low-heat setting for 9 to 10 hours or on high-heat setting for 4½ to 5 hours.
5. Using a slotted spoon, transfer meat to a cutting board. Discard bay leaves. Add salt to mixture in cooker. Using two forks, pull meat apart into shreds; return to cooker, stirring to combine.
6. Preheat broiler. Arrange bread slices on a baking sheet; top each with a cheese slice. Broil 4 to 5 inches from heat until cheese melts and bread is toasted. To serve, using a slotted spoon, divide meat mixture among bread slices.

PER SERVING: 272 cal., 8 g total fat (4 g sat. fat), 31 mg chol., 563 mg sodium, 26 g carb. (4 g fiber, 5 g sugars), 21 g pro. Exchanges: 1.5 starch, 2 lean meat, 0.5 vegetable, 1 fat.

- 1 tablespoon instant espresso coffee powder
- 1 pound extra-lean boneless beef chuck roast, trimmed of fat
  Nonstick cooking spray
- 3 medium onions, chopped (1½ cups)
- ½ of a medium red sweet pepper, cut into thin bite-size strips
- ½ of a medium green sweet pepper, cut into thin bite-size trips
- 4 cloves garlic, minced, or 2 teaspoons bottled minced garlic
- 2 bay leaves
- ½ cup dry red wine
- 2 tablespoons cider vinegar
- 1 tablespoon Worcestershire sauce
- ½ teaspoon salt
- 6 thick slices multigrain Italian bread (about 1½ ounces each)
- 6 thin slices provolone cheese (3 ounces total)

Curried Chicken with Naan

38g CARB PER SERVING

PREP: 50 minutes **SLOW COOK:** 7 to 8 hours (low) or 3½ to 4 hours (high) **BAKE:** 10 minutes
MAKES: 6 servings (1 open-face sandwich each)

1. Place sliced onions and carrots in a 3½- or 4-quart slow cooker. In a small bowl combine coriander, cumin, turmeric, salt, cardamom, cinnamon, cayenne pepper, and cloves. Sprinkle evenly over chicken, rubbing in with your fingers. Place chicken on top of vegetables in cooker.

2. Cover and cook on low-heat setting for 7 to 8 hours or on high-heat setting for 3½ to 4 hours.

3. Remove chicken from cooker, reserving vegetable mixture in cooker. Transfer chicken to a cutting board. Let stand until just cool enough to handle. Remove chicken from the bones; discard bones. Coarsely chop chicken. Stir chicken into the vegetable mixture in slow cooker.

4. Meanwhile, preheat oven to 350°F. Stack naan and wrap tightly with foil. Bake for 10 minutes or until warm.

5. Divide naan among six serving plates. Arrange spinach and chopped chicken mixture over naan. To serve, spoon Mango-Ginger Chutney on top. If desired, sprinkle with green onion.

Mango-Ginger Chutney: In a small bowl combine 2 tablespoons chopped raisins and 4 teaspoons rice vinegar; let stand for 10 minutes. Place 1 cup fresh or frozen mango chunks, thawed, in a food processor. Cover and process until coarsely pureed. Add to raisin mixture. Add 2 green onion tops, thinly sliced; 1 teaspoon grated fresh ginger; and ¼ teaspoon salt.

- 2 large onions, halved and thinly sliced
- 4 large carrots, sliced
- ¾ teaspoon ground coriander
- ¾ teaspoon ground cumin
- ½ teaspoon turmeric
- ¼ teaspoon salt
- ¼ teaspoon ground cardamom
- ¼ teaspoon ground cinnamon
- ¼ teaspoon cayenne pepper
- ⅛ teaspoon ground cloves
- 2 to 2½ pounds bone-in chicken thighs, skinned
- 6 small (1½ ounces each) whole wheat naan rounds or whole wheat pita bread rounds
- 4 cups fresh baby spinach
- 1 recipe Mango-Ginger Chutney
  Chopped green onion (optional)

PER SERVING: 288 cal., 6 g total fat (2 g sat. fat), 75 mg chol., 581 mg sodium, 38 g carb. (6 g fiber, 12 g sugars), 23 g pro. Exchanges: 2 starch, 2.5 lean meat, 1 vegetable.

Chicken Panini with Cilantro Mayonnaise

32g CARB PER SERVING

PREP: 30 minutes **SLOW COOK:** 6 to 6½ hours (low) or 3 to 3¼ hours (high) **GRILL:** 2 minutes
MAKES: 6 servings (1 sandwich each)

2   cloves garlic, minced
¼   teaspoon salt
¼   teaspoon black pepper
2   pounds bone-in chicken breast halves, skinned
½   cup water
12   ½-inch-thick slices whole grain Italian or French bread (10 to 12 ounces total)
1   recipe Cilantro Mayonnaise
6   ¼-inch-thick slices fresh pineapple, quartered
2   cups lightly packed fresh baby spinach leaves
    Nonstick cooking spray

1. Sprinkle garlic, salt, and pepper evenly over chicken, rubbing in with your fingers. Place chicken pieces in a 3½- or 4-quart slow cooker. Add the water to cooker.

2. Cover and cook on low-heat setting for 6 to 6½ hours or on high-heat setting for 3 to 3¼ hours. Remove chicken from cooker. Let stand until just cool enough to handle. Remove chicken from the bones; discard bones. Using two forks, coarsely shred chicken.

3. Spread half of the bread slices with Cilantro Mayonnaise. Divide chicken among the spread bread slices. Top chicken with pineapple and spinach leaves. Top with remaining bread slices. Coat both sides of sandwiches with cooking spray (sandwiches will be full).

4. Lightly coat an unheated panini griddle, covered indoor electric grill, or large nonstick skillet with cooking spray. Heat griddle or grill according to manufacturer's directions. (Or preheat skillet over medium heat.) If necessary, add sandwiches in batches. If using griddle or grill, close lid and cook for 2 to 3 minutes or until bread is toasted. (If using skillet, place a heavy plate on top of sandwiches. Cook for 1 to 2 minutes or until bottoms are toasted. Carefully remove plate, which may be hot. Turn sandwiches and top with the plate. Cook for 1 to 2 minutes more or until bread is toasted.) Cut sandwiches in half to serve.

Cilantro Mayonnaise: In a small bowl combine ⅓ cup light mayonnaise, ¼ cup snipped fresh cilantro, 2 tablespoons honey mustard, and ½ teaspoon finely shredded lime peel.

PER SERVING: 331 cal., 8 g total fat (1 g sat. fat), 68 mg chol., 504 mg sodium, 32 g carb. (3 g fiber, 9 g sugars), 29 g pro. Exchanges: 2 starch, 3 lean meat, 1 vegetable, 0.5 fat.

Turkey Reubens

28g
CARB PER SERVING

PREP: 15 minutes **SLOW COOK:** 7 to 8 hours (low) or 3½ to 4 hours (high), plus 30 minutes (high) **BROIL:** 2 minutes
MAKES: 6 servings (1 open-face sandwich each)

1. Place celery and onion in a 3½- or 4-quart slow cooker. Add the water to cooker. In a small bowl combine caraway seeds, celery seeds, salt, and pepper. Sprinkle evenly over turkey. Place turkey on celery and onions in cooker.
2. Cover and cook on low-heat setting for 7 to 8 hours or on high-heat setting for 3½ to 4 hours. If using low-heat setting, turn to high-heat setting. Add cabbage and carrots to cooker; cover and cook for 30 minutes more.
3. Preheat broiler. Using tongs, remove cabbage and carrots from cooker; set aside. Transfer turkey to a cutting board; remove and discard skin and bones. Thinly slice or shred turkey. Discard celery and onion from cooker. Place bread slices on a large baking sheet. Broil 3 to 4 inches from the heat for 1 to 2 minutes or until tops are lightly toasted. Turn bread slices over and top each with a slice of cheese. Broil 1 to 2 minutes more or until cheese is melted.
4. Place ¾ cup turkey and ¾ cup cabbage mixture on each cheese-topped bread slice. Top each sandwich with about 1 tablespoon of the salad dressing.

PER SERVING: 341 cal., 8 g total fat (3 g sat. fat), 86 mg chol., 591 mg sodium, 28 g carb. (4 g fiber, 8 g sugars), 41 g pro. Exchanges: 1 starch, 5 lean meat, 2 vegetable.

- 2 **stalks celery, cut crosswise into thirds**
- 1 **medium onion, cut into wedges**
- 1 **cup water**
- ½ **teaspoon caraway seeds, crushed**
- ¼ **teaspoon celery seeds**
- ¼ **teaspoon salt**
- ¼ **teaspoon black pepper**
- 2 **to 2½ pounds bone-in turkey breast halves**
- 6 **cups shredded fresh cabbage**
- 2 **cups purchased coarsely shredded carrots**
- 6 **slices rye bread**
- 6 **¾-ounce slices reduced-fat Swiss cheese**
- ½ **cup bottled reduced-calorie Thousand Island salad dressing**

Cook Well: Regular green cabbage tastes great in these sandwiches. These two top-notch varieties are also worth a try:

- **Savoy cabbage:** Sometimes called curly cabbage, this variety gets thumbs-up from cooks for its lovely lacy leaves and mild flavor.
- **Chinese cabbage:** Also known as napa cabbage, this variety adds a slightly peppery kick to recipes.

Chicken Tostadas

22g CARB PER SERVING

PREP: 25 minutes **SLOW COOK:** 5 to 6 hours (low) or 2½ to 3 hours (high)
MAKES: 10 servings (1 tostada each)

 2 **fresh jalapeño chile peppers, seeded and finely chopped***
 8 **cloves garlic, minced**
 3 **tablespoons chili powder**
 3 **tablespoons lime juice**
 ¼ **teaspoon bottled hot pepper sauce**
 1 **medium onion, sliced and separated into rings**
 2 **pounds skinless, boneless chicken thighs**
 1 **16-ounce can fat-free refried beans**
 10 **purchased tostada shells**
 ¾ **cup shredded reduced-fat cheddar cheese (3 ounces)**
 2 **cups shredded lettuce**
 ¾ **cup bottled salsa**
 ¾ **cup light sour cream**
 ½ **cup sliced ripe olives Lime wedges (optional)**

1. In a 3½- to 5-quart slow cooker combine jalapeño peppers, garlic, chili powder, lime juice, and hot pepper sauce. Add onion and chicken to cooker.
2. Cover and cook on low-heat setting for 5 to 6 hours or on high-heat setting for 2½ to 3 hours.
3. Remove chicken and onion from cooker, reserving ½ cup of the cooking liquid. Using two forks, shred chicken. In a medium bowl combine chicken, onion, and the ½ cup cooking liquid.
4. Spread refried beans on tostada shells. Top with hot chicken mixture and shredded cheese. Serve with lettuce, salsa, sour cream, and olives. If desired, serve with lime wedges.

*Test Kitchen Tip: Because chile peppers contain volatile oils that can burn your skin and eyes, avoid direct contact with them as much as possible. When working with chile peppers, wear plastic or rubber gloves. If your bare hands do touch the peppers, wash your hands and nails well with soap and warm water.

PER SERVING: 285 cal., 11 g total fat (4 g sat. fat), 86 mg chol., 606 mg sodium, 22 g carb. (5 g fiber, 2 g sugars), 25 g pro. Exchanges: 1.5 starch, 3 lean meat, 1 fat.

Sloppy Pizza Joes

27 g CARB PER SERVING

PREP: 25 minutes **SLOW COOK:** 6 to 8 hours (low) or 3 to 4 hours (high)
MAKES: 16 servings (1 sandwich each)

Nonstick cooking spray
3 **pounds uncooked ground turkey breast**
2 **14-ounce jars pizza sauce**
2 **cups frozen stir-fry vegetables (yellow, red, and green peppers and onions), thawed and drained**
½ **of a 6-ounce can no-salt-added tomato paste (⅓ cup)**
16 **whole wheat hamburger buns, split and toasted***
8 **1-ounce slices part-skim mozzarella cheese, halved**
¼ **cup sliced pitted ripe olives (optional)**
Snipped fresh basil (optional)

1. Coat an unheated extra-large skillet with cooking spray; heat over medium-high heat. Cook half of the turkey at a time until no longer pink, stirring to break up turkey as it cooks. In a 4- to 5-quart slow cooker stir together turkey, pizza sauce, vegetables, and tomato paste.
2. Cover and cook on low-heat setting for 6 to 8 hours or on high-heat setting for 3 to 4 hours.
3. Spoon about ½ cup turkey mixture onto each bun bottom. Top each with a half slice of cheese and, if desired, olives and basil. Add bun tops.

***Test Kitchen Tip:** To toast buns, arrange split buns, cut sides up, on an unheated broiler pan. Broil 3 to 4 inches from the heat for 1 to 2 minutes or until toasted.

PER SERVING: 276 cal., 4 g total fat (2 g sat. fat), 63 mg chol., 438 mg sodium, 27 g carb. (3 g fiber, 6 g sugars), 30 g pro. Exchanges: 2 starch, 3.5 lean meat.

Cook Well: Options for part-skim mozzarella include reduced-fat versions of other cheeses, including American, cheddar, Monterey Jack, pepper Jack, Colby-Jack, provolone, and Muenster.

Because they have less fat, reduced-fat cheeses do not always melt to the same oozy consistency as regular cheeses; however, if you place thin slices on hot food, they should soften nicely and provide that extra boost of flavor cheese adds.

Sausage Sandwiches with Roasted Veggies

36g CARB PER SERVING

PREP: 10 minutes **SLOW COOK:** 6½ to 7 hours (low) or 3 to 3½ hours (high)
MAKES: 4 servings (1 sandwich each)

1. Coat an unheated 3- to 4-quart slow cooker with cooking spray. In a medium nonstick skillet heat 1 teaspoon of the oil over medium heat; add sausage. Cook until browned on all sides, turning links frequently.
2. Add the remaining 1 teaspoon oil, the sweet pepper, onion, tomatoes, garlic, and oregano to slow cooker, tossing until combined. Arrange sausages on top of mixture in cooker.
3. Cover and cook on low-heat setting for 6½ to 7 hours or on high-heat setting for 3 to 3½ hours.
4. Meanwhile, for sauce, in a small bowl whisk together mayonnaise and mustard; cover with plastic wrap. Chill until serving time.
5. To serve, spoon about ⅓ cup of the vegetable mixture into each bun. Cut each sausage piece in half lengthwise; place each half, cut side down, on top of vegetables. Spoon the sauce over sausage.

PER SERVING: 308 cal., 12 g total fat (3 g sat. fat), 34 mg chol., 596 mg sodium, 36 g carb. (3 g fiber, 11 g sugars), 13 g pro. Exchanges: 2 starch, 1 medium-fat meat, 0.5 vegetable, 1 fat.

Nonstick cooking spray
2 **teaspoons olive oil**
2 **chicken-apple sausage links or two 4-inch pieces smoked turkey sausage**
1 **medium green sweet pepper, sliced**
1 **medium onion, cut into 12 wedges**
1 **cup grape tomatoes**
4 **cloves garlic, minced**
1 **teaspoon dried oregano, crushed**
3 **tablespoons light mayonnaise or salad dressing**
2 **teaspoons honey mustard**
4 **whole wheat hot dog buns, lightly toasted**

Saucy Meatball Sandwiches

34g CARB PER SERVING

PREP: 45 minutes **SLOW COOK:** 4 to 5 hours (low) or 2 to 2½ hours (high) **BROIL:** 1 minute
MAKES: 10 servings (1 sandwich each)

2 small onions
1½ cups finely chopped fresh mushrooms
½ cup refrigerated or frozen egg product, thawed, or 2 eggs, lightly beaten
⅓ cup fine dry bread crumbs
¼ teaspoon black pepper
⅛ teaspoon salt
2 pounds ground turkey breast
4 ounces thinly sliced cooked lower-sodium ham, chopped
3 medium red sweet peppers, quartered
1 14.5-ounce can no-salt-added diced tomatoes, undrained
10 3-ounce portions whole grain baguette-style French bread, split
Fresh basil leaves (optional)
5 ¾-ounce slices reduced-fat Swiss cheese, halved

1. Finely chop one of the onions. Cut the other onion into thin wedges. Set both aside. For meatballs, in a large bowl combine finely chopped onion, mushrooms, egg, bread crumbs, black pepper, and salt. Add ground turkey and ham; mix well. Using slightly wet hands, shape mixture into thirty 2-inch meatballs. Coat an extra-large unheated nonstick skillet with *nonstick cooking spray*; heat over medium heat. Cook meatballs, half at a time, in hot skillet until evenly browned, turning occasionally.

2. In a 5- to 6-quart slow cooker combine onion wedges, pepper quarters, and tomatoes. Place meatballs on mixture in cooker.

3. Cover and cook on low-heat setting for 4 to 5 hours or on high-heat setting for 2 to 2½ hours.

4. Remove meatballs from cooker with a slotted spoon; keep warm. Using the slotted spoon, transfer onions, peppers, and tomatoes to a blender or food processor; discard remaining cooking liquid in cooker. Cover and blend or process pepper mixture until smooth.

5. Preheat broiler. Remove centers from bread portions.* Place bread portions, cut sides up, on a large baking sheet. Broil 3 to 4 inches from the heat for 1 to 2 minutes or until lightly toasted.

6. If desired, arrange basil leaves on bottom halves of bread portions; add three meatballs to each. Top each with 3 tablespoons sauce and a half slice of cheese. Remove remaining bread tops from the pan. Broil sandwiches for 30 to 60 seconds or until cheese is melted. Add bread tops and serve warm.

*Test Kitchen Tip:** After removing bread centers, the remaining sandwich portions should be 2 ounces each. Reserve bread centers to use as soft bread crumbs in other recipes.

PER SERVING: 342 cal., 7 g total fat (2 g sat. fat), 58 mg chol., 546 mg sodium, 34 g carb. (4 g fiber, 6 g sugars), 34 g pro. Exchanges: 2 starch, 4 lean meat, 1 vegetable.

Eggplant Parmesan Sandwich Stacks

31g CARB PER SERVING

PREP: 20 minutes **SLOW COOK:** 3½ hours (low) **BROIL:** 1 minute
MAKES: 8 servings (1 sandwich each)

1. Lightly coat an unheated 3½- or 4-quart slow cooker with cooking spray. Place mushrooms in the prepared cooker. Top with eggplant. In a medium bowl combine pasta sauce, tomato paste, garlic, and Italian seasoning. Pour over all in cooker.
2. Cover and cook on low-heat setting for 3 to 3½ hours.
3. Preheat broiler. Place sandwich thin bottoms and tops, cut sides up, on a large baking sheet. Place a mozzarella slice on cut side of each sandwich thin bottom. Broil 3 to 4 inches from the heat for 1 to 3 minutes or until bread is toasted and cheese is just melted.
4. To serve, place toasted sandwich thin bottoms on eight serving plates. Remove eggplant slices from cooker and place on top of cheese. Stir mushroom mixture in cooker and spoon on top of eggplant slices. Top with basil leaves and sandwich thin tops. Serve with a knife and fork.

PER SERVING: 225 cal., 8 g total fat (4 g sat. fat), 20 mg chol., 425 mg sodium, 31 g carb. (8 g fiber, 7 g sugars), 12 g pro. Exchanges: 2 starch, 1 lean meat, 0.5 fat.

Nonstick cooking spray
2 cups sliced fresh mushrooms
8 1-inch-thick eggplant slices
1 cup light tomato-basil pasta sauce
1 6-ounce can no-salt-added tomato paste
3 cloves garlic, minced
1 teaspoon dried Italian seasoning, crushed
8 whole wheat sandwich thins, split
8 ounces fresh mozzarella cheese, cut into 8 slices
16 large fresh basil leaves

Lemony Lamb Pitas

PREP: 30 minutes **SLOW COOK:** 8 to 10 hours (low) or 4 to 5 hours (high)
MAKES: 8 servings (1 filled pita half each)

1 large onion, sliced
½ teaspoon lemon-pepper seasoning
½ teaspoon dry mustard
1 2-pound boneless lamb leg roast, trimmed of fat
½ cup chicken broth
¼ teaspoon finely shredded lemon peel
1 tablespoon lemon juice
1 teaspoon snipped fresh rosemary or ¼ teaspoon dried rosemary, crushed
2 cloves garlic, minced
4 large whole wheat pita bread rounds, halved crosswise
8 lettuce leaves
1 recipe Yogurt Sauce
1 small tomato, seeded and chopped

1. Place onion in a 3½- or 4-quart slow cooker. Combine lemon-pepper seasoning and dry mustard. Sprinkle mixture over roast; rub in with your fingers. Place roast in cooker. In a small bowl combine broth, lemon peel, lemon juice, rosemary, and garlic. Pour over all in cooker.

2. Cover and cook on low-heat setting for 8 to 10 hours or on high-heat setting for 4 to 5 hours.

3. Remove meat from cooker. Using two forks, shred meat; discard fat. Place meat in a bowl. Using a slotted spoon, remove onion from cooker and stir into meat. Discard cooking liquid in cooker.

4. To serve, open pita bread halves to form pockets. Place a lettuce leaf in each pita half pocket. Spoon ½ cup meat mixture into each pita half. Top each with 1 tablespoon Yogurt Sauce and 1 tablespoon chopped tomato.

Yogurt Sauce: In a small bowl stir together ½ cup plain low-fat yogurt, ¼ cup chopped and seeded cucumber, and ½ teaspoon lemon-pepper seasoning.

PER SERVING: 293 cal., 7 g total fat (2 g sat. fat), 76 mg chol., 515 mg sodium, 28 g carb. (4 g fiber, 3 g sugars), 29 g pro. Exchanges: 1.5 starch, 3.5 lean meat, 1 vegetable.

satisfying sides

When it's your turn to host, fill your slow cooker with one of these nutritious side dishes. Each will satisfy a crowd and keep the stove top and oven clear for cooking the rest of your feast.

Slow-"Roasted" Tomatoes

13g CARB PER SERVING

PREP: 15 minutes **SLOW COOK:** 2 hours (low) or 1 hour (high) **STAND:** 10 minutes
MAKES: 4 servings (1 tomato half each)

Nonstick cooking spray
2 large very firm underripe tomatoes (about 10 ounces each), halved crosswise
1 tablespoon balsamic vinegar
2 teaspoons olive oil
2 cloves garlic, minced
1 teaspoon dried basil, crushed
½ teaspoon dried oregano, crushed
¼ teaspoon dried rosemary, crushed
⅛ teaspoon salt
¾ cup coarse soft whole wheat bread crumbs (1 slice)
2 tablespoons grated Parmesan cheese
Snipped fresh basil (optional)

1. Lightly coat an unheated 3- or 3½-quart slow cooker with cooking spray. Place tomatoes, cut sides up, in bottom of slow cooker. In a small bowl combine vinegar, olive oil, garlic, dried basil, oregano, rosemary, and salt. Spoon evenly over tomatoes in cooker.

2. Cover and cook on low-heat setting for 2 hours or on high-heat setting for 1 hour.

3. Preheat a medium nonstick skillet over medium-high heat. Add the bread crumbs and cook for 2 to 3 minutes or until lightly browned, stirring constantly. Remove from heat; stir in Parmesan cheese.

4. To serve, remove tomatoes from cooker and place on a serving platter. Drizzle cooking liquid evenly over the tomatoes. Sprinkle with the bread crumb mixture. Let stand for 10 minutes to absorb flavors. If desired, garnish with snipped fresh basil.

PER SERVING: 96 cal., 4 g total fat (1 g sat. fat), 2 mg chol., 159 mg sodium, 13 g carb. (3 g fiber, 5 g sugars), 3 g pro. Exchanges: 2 vegetable, 1 fat.

Slow-Cooked Sweet and Sour Cabbage

17 g CARB PER SERVING

PREP: 25 minutes **SLOW COOK:** 4 to 5 hours (low) or 2 to 2½ hours (high)
MAKES: 6 servings (¾ cup each)

6 cups shredded red cabbage (1 small head)
2 large apples, chopped (2 cups)
¼ cup cider vinegar
¼ cup water
3 tablespoons packed dark brown sugar*
1 tablespoon canola oil
1½ teaspoons dried thyme, crushed
¼ teaspoon salt
¼ teaspoon black pepper
⅛ teaspoon ground cloves

1. In a 3½- or 4-quart slow cooker combine the cabbage, apples, vinegar, water, brown sugar, oil, thyme, salt, pepper, and cloves. Mix well.

2. Cover and cook on low-heat setting for 4 to 5 hours or on high-heat setting for 2 to 2½ hours. Stir before serving.

*Sugar Substitute: We do not recommend using a sugar substitute for this recipe.

PER SERVING: 90 cal., 2 g total fat (0 g sat. fat), 0 mg chol., 119 mg sodium, 17 g carb. (3 g fiber, 13 g sugars), 1 g pro. Exchanges: 0.5 fruit, 1 vegetable, 0.5 fat.

Time-Saving Trick: To save on prep time, look for shredded red cabbage in the produce aisle. However, shredding it yourself takes just a few minutes. Here's how:

- Just before using, remove and discard any outer leaves that are shriveled, damaged, or darkened.
- Rinse the cabbage in cold water. Pat it dry.
- Using a large chef's knife, cut the cabbage into wedges; remove and discard the tough core from each wedge.
- Thinly slice the cored cabbage wedge across the grain of the leaves.

Sweet Ginger Roots

28g
CARB PER SERVING

PREP: 15 minutes **SLOW COOK:** 6 hours (low) or 3 hours (high), plus 20 minutes (high)
MAKES: 8 servings (¾ cup each)

1. In a 3½- or 4-quart slow cooker combine the beets, carrots, ginger, juice, and salt.
2. Cover and cook on low-heat setting for 6 hours or high-heat setting for 3 hours. If using low-heat setting, turn to high-heat setting. Stir together the cornstarch and cold water. Stir into beet mixture with the sugar or sugar substitute. Cover and cook for 20 minutes more or until thickened and bubbly.

*Test Kitchen Tip: To peel beets easily, use a vegetable peeler and peel the beets under slow running water. The water helps to prevent the beets from staining your fingertips. Wear plastic or rubber gloves if you wish.

**Sugar Substitutes: Choose from Splenda Granular or Sweet'N Low bulk or packets. Follow package directions to use product amount equivalent to ¼ cup sugar.

PER SERVING: 122 cal., 0 g total fat, 0 mg chol., 225 mg sodium, 28 g carb. (6 g fiber, 21 g sugars), 3 g pro. Exchanges: 1.5 carb., 1 vegetable.

PER SERVING WITH SUBSTITUTE: Same as above, except 100 cal., 23 g carb. (15 g sugars). Exchanges: 1 carb.

2¾ **pounds red and/or golden beets, trimmed, peeled, and cut into ¾-inch wedges***
12 **ounces carrots, peeled and cut into 3-inch pieces (halve any thick pieces) (4 medium)**
2 **teaspoons grated fresh ginger**
½ **cup pomegranate juice**
¼ **teaspoon salt**
1 **tablespoon cornstarch**
1 **tablespoon cold water**
¼ **cup sugar****

Cheesy Sweet Peppers and Corn

19g CARB PER SERVING

PREP: 20 minutes SLOW COOK: 3 hours (low) or 1½ hours (high), plus 10 minutes (high)
MAKES: 6 servings (½ cup each)

1. Lightly coat an unheated 3- or 3½-quart slow cooker with cooking spray. Add corn, sweet peppers, green onions, and the water to cooker.
2. Cover and cook on low-heat setting for 3 hours or on high-heat setting for 1½ hours.
3. If using low-heat setting, turn to high-heat setting. In a small bowl whisk together half-and-half and cornstarch until cornstarch is dissolved. Stir into the vegetable mixture in cooker. Cover and cook for 10 minutes more or until thickened. Stir in blue cheese, ½ teaspoon black pepper, and the salt. Spoon into a shallow serving bowl; sprinkle with cheddar cheese. If desired, sprinkle with additional black pepper.

PER SERVING: 121 cal., 3 g total fat (2 g sat. fat), 8 mg chol., 237 mg sodium, 19 g carb. (2 g fiber, 3 g sugars), 6 g pro. Exchanges: 1 starch, 1 vegetable, 0.5 fat.

Nonstick cooking spray
1 16-ounce package frozen whole kernel corn
½ cup diced red sweet pepper
½ cup diced green sweet pepper
¼ cup finely chopped green onions
¼ cup water
¼ cup fat-free half-and-half
2 teaspoons cornstarch
1 ounce crumbled reduced-fat blue cheese
½ teaspoon coarsely ground black pepper
¼ teaspoon salt
1½ ounces shredded reduced-fat sharp cheddar cheese
  Coarsely ground black pepper (optional)

Hot German-Style Potato Salad

PREP: 25 minutes **SLOW COOK:** 8 to 9 hours (low) or 4 to 4½ hours (high)
MAKES: 12 servings (½ cup each)

6 **cups potatoes cut into ¾-inch cubes**
1 **large onion, chopped (1 cup)**
1 **cup water**
⅔ **cup cider vinegar**
¼ **cup packed brown sugar***
2 **tablespoons quick-cooking tapioca, crushed**
½ **teaspoon salt**
¼ **teaspoon celery seeds**
¼ **teaspoon black pepper**
4 **slices turkey bacon, cooked according to package directions and chopped**
   Sliced green onions (optional)

1. In a 3½- or 4-quart slow cooker combine potatoes and onion. In a medium bowl combine the water, vinegar, brown sugar, tapioca, salt, celery seeds, and pepper; pour over all in cooker.
2. Cover and cook on low-heat setting for 8 to 9 hours or on high-heat setting for 4 to 4½ hours. Just before serving, stir in bacon. If desired, sprinkle with sliced green onions.

*Sugar Substitute: We do not recommend using a sugar substitute for this recipe.

PER SERVING: 100 cal., 1 g total fat (0 g sat. fat), 5 mg chol., 163 mg sodium, 21 g carb. (1 g fiber, 6 g sugars), 2 g pro. Exchanges: 1 starch, 1 vegetable.

Garlic Mashed Potatoes

21g CARB PER SERVING

PREP: 25 minutes **SLOW COOK:** 6 to 8 hours (low) or 3 to 4 hours (high)
MAKES: 12 servings (½ cup each)

1. In a 3½- or 4-quart slow cooker combine potatoes, garlic, and bay leaf. Pour broth over all in cooker.
2. Cover and cook on low-heat setting for 6 to 8 hours or on high-heat setting for 3 to 4 hours.
3. Drain potatoes in a colander over a bowl to catch cooking liquid. Discard bay leaf. Return potatoes to slow cooker. Mash to desired consistency with a potato masher.
4. In a small saucepan heat milk and butter until steaming and butter is almost melted. Add milk mixture, white pepper, salt, and enough of the reserved cooking liquid to the potato mixture to reach desired consistency. Stir in snipped chives. Reserve remaining cooking liquid.* If desired, garnish each serving with whole chives.

*Test Kitchen Tip: If desired, return mashed potato mixture to slow cooker; keep warm on low-heat or warm-heat setting for up to 2 hours. If mixture has thickened, stir in some of the reserved cooking liquid to reach desired consistency.

3 **pounds russet potatoes, peeled and cut into 2-inch pieces**
6 **cloves garlic, halved**
1 **bay leaf**
2 **14.5-ounce cans reduced-sodium chicken broth**
1 **cup fat-free milk**
1 **tablespoon butter**
½ **teaspoon ground white pepper**
¼ **teaspoon salt**
¼ **cup snipped fresh chives**
  Whole fresh chives (optional)

PER SERVING: 104 cal., 1 g total fat (1 g sat. fat), 3 mg chol., 226 mg sodium, 21 g carb. (1 g fiber, 3 g sugars), 3 g pro. Exchanges: 1.5 starch.

Caramelized Onions and Potatoes

25g CARB PER SERVING

PREP: 15 minutes **SLOW COOK:** 6 to 7 hours (low) or 3 to 3½ hours (high)
MAKES: 8 servings (½ cup each)

2 **large sweet onions (such as Vidalia, Maui, or Walla Walla), thinly sliced (2 cups)**
1½ **pounds tiny new potatoes, halved**
½ **cup lower-sodium beef broth or reduced-sodium chicken broth**
2 **tablespoons butter, melted**
1 **to 2 tablespoons packed brown sugar***
¼ **teaspoon salt**
¼ **teaspoon black pepper**
   Black pepper (optional)
   Snipped fresh chives (optional)

1. In a 3½- or 4-quart slow cooker combine onions and potatoes.
2. In a small bowl combine broth, butter, brown sugar, salt, and the ¼ teaspoon pepper. Pour mixture over all in cooker.
3. Cover and cook on low-heat setting for 6 to 7 hours or on high-heat setting for 3 to 3½ hours. Stir gently before serving. Serve with a slotted spoon. If desired, spoon some of the cooking liquid over potatoes to moisten and sprinkle with additional pepper and/or snipped fresh chives.

*Sugar Substitutes:** Choose from Sweet'N Low Brown or Sugar Twin Granulated Brown. Follow package directions to use product amount equivalent to 1 to 2 tablespoons brown sugar.

PER SERVING: 134 cal., 3 g total fat (2 g sat. fat), 8 mg chol., 140 mg sodium, 25 g carb. (3 g fiber, 8 g sugars), 3 g pro. Exchanges: 1.5 starch, 0.5 fat.

PER SERVING WITH SUBSTITUTE: Same as above, except 127 cal., 139 mg sodium, 23 g carb. (6 g sugars).

Maple-Ginger Sweet Potatoes

23 g CARB PER SERVING

PREP: 25 minutes **SLOW COOK:** 5 to 6 hours (low) or 2½ to 3 hours (high)
MAKES: 8 servings (½ cup each)

1. In a 3½- or 4-quart slow cooker combine sweet potatoes, apples, dried cranberries, ginger, salt, cinnamon, nutmeg, and pepper. Pour the water and syrup over all in cooker.
2. Cover and cook on low-heat setting for 5 to 6 hours or on high-heat setting for 2½ to 3 hours.

PER SERVING: 92 cal., 0 g total fat, 0 mg chol., 194 mg sodium, 23 g carb. (3 g fiber, 10 g sugars), 1 g pro. Exchanges: 1 starch, 0.5 fruit.

1½ **pounds sweet potatoes, peeled and cut into bite-size pieces (about 5 cups)**
2 **medium tart cooking apples, cored and coarsely chopped (about 2 cups)**
¼ **cup dried cranberries**
1½ **teaspoons grated fresh ginger**
½ **teaspoon salt**
½ **teaspoon ground cinnamon**
¼ **teaspoon ground nutmeg**
⅛ **teaspoon black pepper**
½ **cup water**
¼ **cup light pancake syrup**

Cook Well: Some apples hold up well in cooking; others don't. Pleasingly tart Granny Smith apples are a terrific choice for cooking. For a mildly tart cooking apple, opt for Rome Beauty apples. For sweet-tart cooking choices, reach for Braeburn, Jonagold, and Jonathan varieties.

Barley Risotto with Butternut Squash

27 g
CARB PER SERVING

PREP: 25 minutes **SLOW COOK:** 4 to 5 hours (low) or 2 to 2½ hours (high)
MAKES: 12 servings (⅔ cup each)

1. In a 3½- or 4-quart slow cooker stir together the broth, water, butternut squash, barley, leek, thyme, and pepper. Cover and cook on low-heat setting for 4 to 5 hours or on high-heat setting for 2 to 2½ hours.
2. Before serving, stir in ¼ cup cheese, the parsley, and olive oil. If desired, sprinkle with the 4 tablespoons additional cheese.

PER SERVING: 133 cal., 2 g total fat (0 g sat. fat), 1 mg chol., 208 mg sodium, 27 g carb. (5 g fiber, 2 g sugars), 4 g pro. Exchanges: 2 starch.

- 2 **14.5-ounce cans reduced-sodium chicken broth**
- 1⅓ **cups water**
- 1 **1½-pound butternut squash, peeled, seeded, and chopped (4 cups)**
- 1½ **cups regular pearl barley**
- 1 **medium leek, halved and thinly sliced (⅓ cup)**
- ½ **teaspoon dried thyme, crushed**
- ¼ **teaspoon black pepper**
- ¼ **cup finely shredded Parmigiano-Reggiano cheese or Parmesan cheese**
- ¼ **cup snipped fresh parsley**
- 2 **teaspoons olive oil**
- 4 **tablespoons finely shredded Parmigiano-Reggiano cheese or Parmesan cheese (optional)**

Cook Well: The leek, a mild-tasting cousin of onions and garlic, looks like an overgrown green onion. Leeks add a mellow, oniony appeal to recipes.

Choose leeks that are 1½ inches or smaller in diameter—they'll be more tender than larger leeks. To clean and cut leeks:

- Using a chef's knife, cut and discard a thin slice from the root end of the leek. Cut off and discard the dark green leaves from the top of the stalk. Remove and discard any wilted outer leaves.
- Cut the remaining leek lengthwise, from top to bottom.
- Hold each leek half under the faucet with the root ends up. Rinse under cool running water, separating and lifting the leaves with your fingers to remove all the sand and grit.
- Thinly slice the leeks crosswise or as directed in your recipe.

Multigrain Pilaf

24g CARB PER SERVING

PREP: 20 minutes **SLOW COOK:** 6 to 8 hours (low) or 3 to 4 hours (high)
MAKES: 12 servings (⅔ cup each)

⅔ **cup uncooked wheat berries**

½ **cup uncooked regular barley (not quick-cooking)**

½ **cup uncooked wild rice**

2 **14.5-ounce cans reduced-sodium vegetable broth or reduced-sodium chicken broth**

2 **cups frozen sweet soybeans (edamame) or baby lima beans**

1 **medium red sweet pepper, chopped (¾ cup)**

1 **medium onion, finely chopped (½ cup)**

1 **tablespoon butter**

¾ **teaspoon dried sage, crushed**

¼ **teaspoon coarsely ground black pepper**

4 **cloves garlic, minced**

1. Rinse and drain wheat berries, barley, and wild rice. In a 3½- or 4-quart slow cooker combine wheat berries, barley, wild rice, broth, soybeans, sweet pepper, onion, butter, sage, black pepper, and garlic.

2. Cover and cook on low-heat setting for 6 to 8 hours or on high-heat setting for 3 to 4 hours. Stir before serving.

PER SERVING: 147 cal., 3 g total fat (1 g sat. fat), 3 mg chol., 173 mg sodium, 24 g carb. (5 g fiber, 3 g sugars), 7 g pro. Exchanges: 1.5 starch, 0.5 lean meat.

Curried Acorn Squash

32g CARB PER SERVING

PREP: 15 minutes **SLOW COOK:** 4 hours (low) or 2 hours (high)
MAKES: 4 servings (1 squash wedge and about ⅓ cup topping each)

1. Cut squash into four wedges. Discard stem, seeds, and strings. Lightly coat an unheated 3½- or 4-quart slow cooker with cooking spray. In cooker combine onion, cherries, broth, brown sugar, curry powder, cumin, and salt. Place squash wedges, cut sides down, on top of onion mixture, making sure that an edge of each squash wedge touches the onion mixture.

2. Cover and cook on low-heat setting for 4 hours or on high-heat setting for 2 hours or until the squash is tender when pierced with a fork.

3. Place squash wedges on serving plates. Stir vegetable oil spread and vanilla into onion mixture in cooker. To serve, top each squash wedge with onion mixture and 1 tablespoon yogurt. If desired, sprinkle with ground cinnamon.

*Sugar Substitutes: Choose from Sweet'N Low Brown or Sugar Twin Granulated Brown. Follow package directions to use product amount equivalent to 1 tablespoon brown sugar.

PER SERVING: 158 cal., 3 g total fat (1 g sat. fat), 1 mg chol., 156 mg sodium, 32 g carb., (3 g fiber, 14 g sugars), 3 g pro. Exchanges: 1 starch, 1 fruit, 0.5 fat.

PER SERVING WITH SUBSTITUTE: Same as above, except 145 cal., 155 mg sodium, 29 g carb. (11 g sugars).

1 **large acorn squash (about 1½ pounds)**
  Nonstick cooking spray
1 **medium sweet onion, cut into thin wedges**
¼ **cup dried tart cherries or dried cranberries**
¼ **cup reduced-sodium chicken broth**
1 **tablespoon packed brown sugar***
1 **teaspoon curry powder**
½ **teaspoon ground cumin**
⅛ **teaspoon salt**
1 **tablespoon vegetable oil spread**
2 **teaspoons vanilla**
¼ **cup plain low-fat yogurt**
  Ground cinnamon (optional)

Time-Saving Trick: To make squash easier to cut, pierce it in several places with a fork. Place squash on a paper towel in the microwave. Microwave on 100 percent power (high) for 3 minutes. Handle carefully, using a clean towel to hold the squash in place while cutting.

Herb-Ginger Bulgur

14g CARB PER SERVING

PREP: 15 minutes **SLOW COOK:** 1½ hours (low)
MAKES: 6 servings (½ cup each)

Nonstick cooking spray
¾ cup bulgur, rinsed and drained
1½ cups water
1 medium fresh jalapeño chile pepper, seeded and thinly sliced*
1 tablespoon canola oil
1 tablespoon grated fresh ginger
¼ teaspoon salt
⅓ cup chopped fresh mint or cilantro
1 tablespoon finely shredded lemon peel
Fresh jalapeño chile pepper slices* (optional)
Lemon wedges (optional)

1. Lightly coat an unheated 1½-quart slow cooker with variable heat settings with cooking spray. Add bulgur, the water, the thinly sliced jalapeño, oil, ginger, and salt to the cooker.
2. Cover and cook on low-heat setting for 1½ hours. Stir in mint and lemon peel. Serve hot or at room temperature. If desired, garnish with additional jalapeño slices and lemon wedges.

*Test Kitchen Tip: Because chile peppers contain volatile oils that can burn your skin and eyes, avoid direct contact with them as much as possible. When working with chile peppers, wear plastic or rubber gloves. If your bare hands do touch the peppers, wash your hands and nails well with soap and warm water.

PER SERVING: 83 cal., 3 g total fat (0 g sat. fat), 0 mg chol., 102 mg sodium, 14 g carb. (4 g fiber, 0 g sugars), 2 g pro. Exchanges: 1 starch.

Red Beans and Rice

29 g CARB PER SERVING

PREP: 15 minutes **COOK:** 10 minutes **STAND:** 1 hour **SLOW COOK:** 10 hours (low) or 5 hours (high)
MAKES: 8 servings (½ cup each)

1. Rinse beans. In a large saucepan combine beans and the water. Bring to boiling; reduce heat. Simmer, uncovered, for 10 minutes. Remove from heat. Cover and let stand for 1 hour. Drain and rinse beans.
2. In a 3½- or 4-quart slow cooker combine beans, broth, onion, sweet pepper, celery, garlic, oregano, cumin, and cayenne pepper. Mix well.
3. Cover and cook on low-heat setting for 10 hours or on high-heat setting for 5 hours. Stir in rice, cilantro, and lime juice. If desired, serve with lime wedges.

PER SERVING: 150 cal., 1 g total fat (0 g sat. fat), 0 mg chol., 160 mg sodium, 29 g carb. (5 g fiber, 2 g sugars), 7 g pro. Exchanges: 2 starch, 0.5 vegetable.

1 **cup dried red kidney beans**
6 **cups water**
2 **cups reduced-sodium chicken broth or water**
1 **medium sweet onion, chopped (¾ cup)**
1 **medium green or red sweet pepper, chopped (¾ cup)**
1 **stalk celery, sliced (½ cup)**
4 **cloves garlic, minced**
½ **teaspoon dried oregano, crushed**
½ **teaspoon ground cumin**
¼ **teaspoon cayenne pepper**
2 **cups hot cooked brown rice**
¼ **cup snipped fresh cilantro**
¼ **cup lime juice**
  Lime wedges (optional)

sweet endings

Save some wiggle room in your meal plan for dessert (and rich, smooth hot chocolate, too)! Whether you're looking for something fruity, fudgy, lemony tart, or spicy sweet, your slow cooker works like an oven (and like a charm) on these treats.

Lemon-Berry Pudding Cake

PREP: 20 minutes **STAND:** 30 minutes **SLOW COOK:** 2½ to 3 hours (high) **COOL:** 1 hour
MAKES: 6 servings (⅔ cup each)

3 eggs
  Nonstick cooking spray
1 cup fresh blueberries and/
  or fresh red raspberries
1 tablespoon granulated
  sugar*
½ cup granulated sugar*
¼ cup flour
2 teaspoons finely shredded
  lemon peel
¼ teaspoon salt
1 cup fat-free milk
3 tablespoons lemon juice
3 tablespoons tub-style
  vegetable oil spread
  Powdered sugar (optional)

1. Let eggs stand at room temperature for 30 minutes. Meanwhile, coat a 2-quart slow cooker with cooking spray. Place berries in cooker and sprinkle with the 1 tablespoon granulated sugar.

2. For batter, separate eggs. In a medium bowl combine the ½ cup granulated sugar, the flour, lemon peel, and salt. Add milk, lemon juice, vegetable oil spread, and egg yolks. Beat with an electric mixer on low speed until combined. Beat on medium speed for 1 minute.

3. Thoroughly wash beaters. In another bowl beat egg whites with an electric mixer on medium speed until soft peaks form (tips curl). Fold egg whites into batter. Carefully pour batter over berries in cooker, spreading evenly.

4. Cover and cook on high-heat setting for 2½ to 3 hours. If cake begins to look too brown on one side, rotate the crockery liner 180 degrees halfway through cooking. Turn off cooker. If possible, remove crockery liner from cooker; cool, uncovered, on a wire rack for 1 hour before serving. If desired, sprinkle with powdered sugar.

*Sugar Substitute: We do not recommend using a sugar substitute for this recipe.

PER SERVING: 200 cal., 7 g total fat (2 g sat. fat), 107 mg chol., 187 mg sodium, 29 g carb. (1 g fiber, 24 g sugars), 5 g pro. Exchanges: 2 carb., 0.5 medium-fat meat, 1 fat.

Rice Pudding with Apricots and a Cherry Swirl

28g CARB PER SERVING

PREP: 20 minutes **SLOW COOK:** 4½ hours (low)
MAKES: 16 servings (½ cup each)

Nonstick cooking spray
6½ cups water
1⅓ cups uncooked converted rice (do not substitute long grain rice)
½ cup sugar*
1 cup snipped dried apricots and/or dried cherries
2 tablespoons butter, softened
1 tablespoon vanilla
½ teaspoon ground cardamom
1 6-ounce carton vanilla Greek yogurt
½ cup sugar-free cherry preserves

1. Coat an unheated 3½- or 4-quart slow cooker with cooking spray; set aside. In a large bowl combine the water, uncooked rice, and sugar. Add apricots, butter, vanilla, and cardamom. Stir well to combine. Transfer to prepared slow cooker.
2. Cover and cook on low-heat setting for 4½ hours (do not stir). Turn off heat; stir in yogurt.
3. Meanwhile, in a small saucepan heat cherry preserves until melted (or place in a small microwave-safe bowl and microwave on 100 percent power [high] for 30 seconds).
4. Stir warm rice pudding and spoon into bowls. Top each serving with 1 to 2 teaspoons cherry preserves. If desired, use a knife to gently swirl in the preserves. Serve warm.

*Sugar Substitute: We do not recommend using a sugar substitute for this recipe.

PER SERVING: 129 cal., 1 g total fat (1 g sat. fat), 4 mg chol., 22 mg sodium, 28 g carb. (1 g fiber, 12 g sugars), 2 g pro. Exchanges: 1 starch, 1 carb.

Fudgy Brownies with Strawberries

23g CARB PER SERVING

PREP: 15 minutes **SLOW COOK:** 2½ hours (high) **COOL:** 30 minutes
MAKES: 12 servings (1 slice brownie, 1 tablespoon dessert topping, and ¼ cup strawberries each)

1. Lightly coat a 1-quart soufflé dish or casserole** with cooking spray. Tear off an 18×12-inch piece of heavy foil; cut in half lengthwise. Fold each piece lengthwise into thirds. Crisscross the foil strips and place the dish in the center of the crisscross; set aside.
2. For batter, in a medium saucepan melt butter and chocolate over low heat. Remove from heat. Stir in eggs, sugar, jam, applesauce, and vanilla. Using a spoon, beat lightly until combined. Stir in flour, baking powder, and salt. Pour batter into prepared dish. Cover dish tightly with foil.
3. Pour the warm water into a 6-quart slow cooker. Using the ends of the foil strips, transfer dish to cooker and leave foil strips under dish.
4. Cover and cook on high-heat setting for 2½ hours or until an instant-read thermometer registers 170°F when inserted in the middle. Using foil strips, carefully remove dish from cooker; discard foil strips. Turn off cooker. If possible, remove crockery liner from cooker. Cool for 30 minutes on a wire rack. Top each serving with dessert topping and, if desired, sprinkle with cocoa powder, serve with strawberries.

*Sugar Substitutes: Choose from C&H Light Sugar and Stevia Blend, Splenda Sugar Blend for Baking, or Sun Crystals Granulated Blend. Follow package directions to use product amount equivalent to ½ cup sugar.

**Test Kitchen Tip: Before beginning this recipe, check to make sure that the dish or casserole you plan to use fits into your slow cooker.

Nonstick cooking spray
¼ cup butter, cut up
2 ounces unsweetened chocolate, chopped
½ cup refrigerated or frozen egg product, thawed, or 2 eggs, lightly beaten
½ cup sugar*
⅓ cup seedless sugar-free strawberry or red raspberry jam
¼ cup unsweetened applesauce
1 teaspoon vanilla
¾ cup flour
¼ teaspoon baking powder
¼ teaspoon salt
1 cup warm water
¾ cup frozen light whipped dessert topping, thawed
3 cups sliced fresh strawberries or raspberries
Unsweetened cocoa powder (optional)

PER SERVING: 153 cal., 7 g total fat (4 g sat. fat), 10 mg chol., 111 mg sodium, 23 g carb. (2 g fiber, 11 g sugars), 3 g pro. Exchanges: 1.5 carb., 1.5 fat.

PER SERVING WITH SUBSTITUTE: Same as above, except 140 cal., 19 g carb. (7 g sugars). Exchanges: 1 carb.

Slow-Cooked Pineapple

15g CARB PER SERVING

PREP: 15 minutes **SLOW COOK:** 3 to 4 hours (low) or 1½ to 2 hours (high)

MAKES: 8 servings (1 pineapple spear, sliced if desired; 3 tablespoons yogurt; ½ tablespoon pistachios; and ½ tablespoon coconut each)

- **1 whole pineapple, peeled**
- **¼ cup water**
- **1 vanilla bean, split lengthwise**
- **1 2- to 3-inch stick cinnamon**
- **2 6-ounce containers fat-free vanilla yogurt**
- **¼ cup coarsely chopped pistachio nuts**
- **¼ cup shredded coconut, toasted**

1. Cut the pineapple lengthwise into eight spears; remove and discard the core from the spears. In a 3- to 4-quart oval slow cooker combine water, vanilla bean, and cinnamon. Add pineapple spears.
2. Cover and cook on low-heat setting for 3 to 4 hours or on high-heat setting for 1½ to 2 hours. Remove and discard the vanilla bean and cinnamon.
3. If desired, slice each pineapple portion into 2 to 3 long slices. Serve pineapple topped with vanilla yogurt, pistachios, and toasted coconut.

PER SERVING: 91 cal., 3 g total fat (1 g sat. fat), 1 mg chol., 30 mg sodium, 15 g carb. (2 g fiber, 10 g sugars), 3 g pro. Exchanges: 1 fruit, 0.5 fat.

Cook Well: Some supermarket produce departments sell peeled, ready-to-slice pineapple, and that's a good option if you're pressed for time.

However, peeling it yourself isn't all that tricky. Here's how:
- Thoroughly rinse the pineapple and scrub with a clean produce brush. Use a knife to cut off the bottom stem end and the green top crown of the fruit.
- Stand the pineapple on one end and slice off the peel in strips from top to bottom. If desired, cut narrow wedge-shape grooves into the pineapple to remove as many "eyes" as possible. Cut the pineapple into spears and core as directed in the recipe.

Cinnamon-Spiced Hot Chocolate

PREP: 10 minutes **SLOW COOK:** 3 to 3½ hours (low)
MAKES: 14 servings (½ cup each)

1. In a 3½- or 4-quart slow cooker combine milk, chocolate pieces, coffee powder, and 1 teaspoon cinnamon.
2. Cover and cook on low-heat setting for 3 to 3½ hours; halfway through cooking, whisk vigorously. Whisk well before serving. If desired, sprinkle each serving with ground cinnamon.

PER SERVING: 140 cal., 8 g total fat (5 g sat. fat), 8 mg chol., 51 mg sodium, 17 g carb. (1 g fiber, 15 g sugars), 4 g pro. Exchanges: 0.5 carb., 0.5 milk, 1.5 fat.

6 cups reduced-fat milk
9 ounces semisweet chocolate pieces
1 teaspoon instant espresso coffee powder
1 teaspoon ground cinnamon
   Ground cinnamon (optional)

Recipe Guide

See how we calculate nutrition information to help you count calories, carbs, and serving sizes.

Nutrition Information

Nutrition facts per serving and food exchanges are noted with each recipe.

Test Kitchen tips and sugar substitutes are listed after the recipe directions.

When ingredient choices appear, we use the first one to calculate the nutrition analysis.

Better Homes and Gardens®

Test Kitchen

High-Standard Testing!

This seal assures you every recipe in this issue of *Diabetic Living® Diabetic Slow Cooker* has been tested in the Better Homes and Gardens® Test Kitchen. This means each recipe is practical, reliable, and meets our high standards of taste appeal.

Precise serving sizes (listed below the recipe title) help you to manage portions.

Kitchen basics such as ice, salt, black pepper, and nonstick cooking spray sometimes are not listed in the ingredient list. In that case, they are italicized in the directions.

Ingredients listed as optional are not included in the per-serving nutrition analysis.

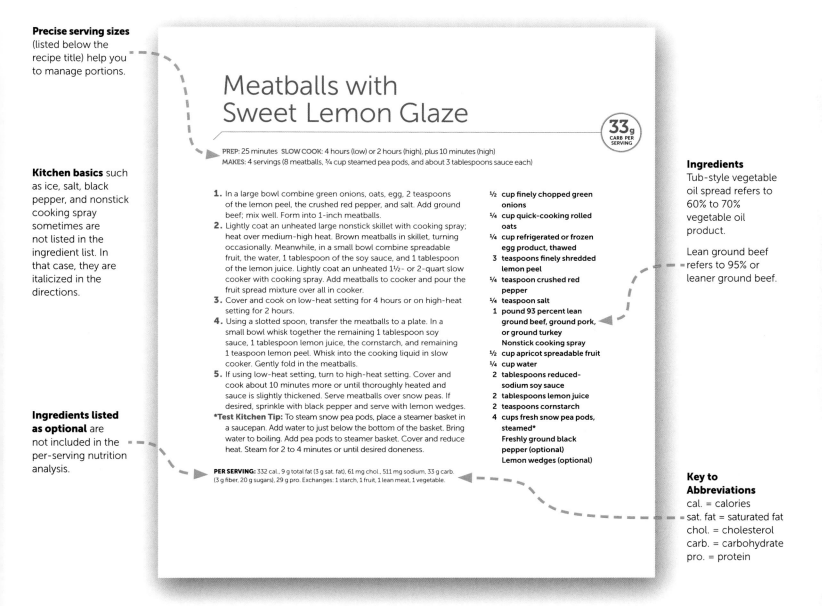

Meatballs with Sweet Lemon Glaze

33g
CARB PER SERVING

PREP: 25 minutes SLOW COOK: 4 hours (low) or 2 hours (high), plus 10 minutes (high)
MAKES: 4 servings (8 meatballs, ¾ cup steamed pea pods, and about 3 tablespoons sauce each)

1. In a large bowl combine green onions, oats, egg, 2 teaspoons of the lemon peel, the crushed red pepper, and salt. Add ground beef; mix well. Form into 1-inch meatballs.
2. Lightly coat an unheated large nonstick skillet with cooking spray; heat over medium-high heat. Brown meatballs in skillet, turning occasionally. Meanwhile, in a small bowl combine spreadable fruit, the water, 1 tablespoon of the soy sauce, and 1 tablespoon of the lemon juice. Lightly coat an unheated 1½- or 2-quart slow cooker with cooking spray. Add meatballs to cooker and pour the fruit spread mixture over all in cooker.
3. Cover and cook on low-heat setting for 4 hours or on high-heat setting for 2 hours.
4. Using a slotted spoon, transfer the meatballs to a plate. In a small bowl whisk together the remaining 1 tablespoon soy sauce, 1 tablespoon lemon juice, the cornstarch, and remaining 1 teaspoon lemon peel. Whisk into the cooking liquid in slow cooker. Gently fold in the meatballs.
5. If using low-heat setting, turn to high-heat setting. Cover and cook about 10 minutes more or until thoroughly heated and sauce is slightly thickened. Serve meatballs over snow peas. If desired, sprinkle with black pepper and serve with lemon wedges.

*Test Kitchen Tip: To steam snow pea pods, place a steamer basket in a saucepan. Add water to just below the bottom of the basket. Bring water to boiling. Add pea pods to steamer basket. Cover and reduce heat. Steam for 2 to 4 minutes or until desired doneness.

PER SERVING: 332 cal., 9 g total fat (3 g sat. fat), 61 mg chol., 511 mg sodium, 33 g carb. (3 g fiber, 20 g sugars), 29 g pro. Exchanges: 1 starch, 1 fruit, 1 lean meat, 1 vegetable.

½ cup finely chopped green onions
¼ cup quick-cooking rolled oats
¼ cup refrigerated or frozen egg product, thawed
3 teaspoons finely shredded lemon peel
¼ teaspoon crushed red pepper
¼ teaspoon salt
1 pound 93 percent lean ground beef, ground pork, or ground turkey
Nonstick cooking spray
½ cup apricot spreadable fruit
¼ cup water
2 tablespoons reduced-sodium soy sauce
2 tablespoons lemon juice
2 teaspoons cornstarch
4 cups fresh snow pea pods, steamed*
Freshly ground black pepper (optional)
Lemon wedges (optional)

Ingredients
Tub-style vegetable oil spread refers to 60% to 70% vegetable oil product.

Lean ground beef refers to 95% or leaner ground beef.

Key to Abbreviations
cal. = calories
sat. fat = saturated fat
chol. = cholesterol
carb. = carbohydrate
pro. = protein

Go to **DiabeticLivingOnline.com** for more diabetes-friendly recipes.

Index

Metric Information

The charts on this page provide a guide for converting measurements from the U.S. customary system, which is used throughout this book, to the metric system.

Product Differences

Most of the ingredients called for in the recipes in this book are available in most countries. However, some are known by different names. Here are some common American ingredients and their possible counterparts:

- Sugar (white) is granulated, fine granulated, or castor sugar.
- Confectioners' sugar is icing sugar.
- All-purpose flour is enriched, bleached, or unbleached white household flour. When self-rising flour is used in place of all-purpose flour in a recipe that calls for leavening, omit the leavening agent (baking soda or baking powder) and salt.
- Light-color corn syrup is golden syrup.
- Cornstarch is cornflour.
- Baking soda is bicarbonate of soda.
- Vanilla or vanilla extract is vanilla essence.
- Green, red, or yellow sweet peppers are capsicums or bell peppers.
- Golden raisins are sultanas.

Volume and Weight

The United States traditionally uses cup measures for liquid and solid ingredients. The chart, bottom right, shows the approximate imperial and metric equivalents. If you are accustomed to weighing solid ingredients, the following approximate equivalents will be helpful.

- 1 cup butter, castor sugar, or rice = 8 ounces = ½ pound = 250 grams
- 1 cup flour = 4 ounces = ¼ pound = 125 grams
- 1 cup icing sugar = 5 ounces = 150 grams

Canadian and U.S. volume for a cup measure is 8 fluid ounces (237 ml), but the standard metric equivalent is 250 ml.

1 British imperial cup is 10 fluid ounces.

In Australia, 1 tablespoon equals 20 ml, and there are 4 teaspoons in the Australian tablespoon.

Spoon measures are used for smaller amounts of ingredients. Although the size of the tablespoon varies slightly in different countries, for practical purposes and for recipes in this book, a straight substitution is all that's necessary. Measurements made using cups or spoons always should be level unless stated otherwise.

Common Weight Range Replacements

IMPERIAL/U.S.	METRIC
½ ounce	15 g
1 ounce	25 g or 30 g
4 ounces (¼ pound)	115 g or 125 g
8 ounces (½ pound)	225 g or 250 g
16 ounces (1 pound)	450 g or 500 g
1¼ pounds	625 g
1½ pounds	750 g
2 pounds or 2¼ pounds	1,000 g or 1 Kg

Oven Temperature Equivalents

FAHRENHEIT SETTING	CELSIUS SETTING*	GAS SETTING
300°F	150°C	Gas Mark 2 (very low)
325°F	160°C	Gas Mark 3 (low)
350°F	180°C	Gas Mark 4 (moderate)
375°F	190°C	Gas Mark 5 (moderate)
400°F	200°C	Gas Mark 6 (hot)
425°F	220°C	Gas Mark 7 (hot)
450°F	230°C	Gas Mark 8 (very hot)
475°F	240°C	Gas Mark 9 (very hot)
500°F	260°C	Gas Mark 10 (extremely hot)
Broil	Broil	Grill

*Electric and gas ovens may be calibrated using Celsius. However, for an electric oven, increase Celsius setting 10 to 20 degrees when cooking above 160°C. For convection or forced-air ovens (gas or electric), lower the temperature setting 25°F/10°C when cooking at all heat levels.

Baking Pan Sizes

IMPERIAL/U.S.	METRIC
9×1½-inch round cake pan	22 or 23×4 cm (1.5 L)
9×1½-inch pie plate	22 or 23×4 cm (1 L)
8×8×2-inch square cake pan	20×5 cm (2 L)
9×9×2-inch square cake pan	22 or 23×4.5 cm (2.5 L)
11×7×1½-inch baking pan	28×17×4 cm (2 L)
2-quart rectangular baking pan	30×19×4.5 cm (3 L)
13×9×2-inch baking pan	34×22×4.5 cm (3.5 L)
15×10×1-inch jelly roll pan	40×25×2 cm
9×5×3-inch loaf pan	23×13×8 cm (2 L)
2-quart casserole	2 L

U.S./Standard Metric Equivalents

⅛ teaspoon = .5 ml	⅓ cup = 3 fluid ounces = 75 ml
¼ teaspoon = 1 ml	½ cup = 4 fluid ounces = 125 ml
½ teaspoon = 2 ml	⅔ cup = 5 fluid ounces = 150 ml
1 teaspoon = 5 ml	¾ cup = 6 fluid ounces = 175 ml
1 tablespoon = 15 ml	1 cup = 8 fluid ounces = 250 ml
2 tablespoons = 25 ml	2 cups = 1 pint = 500 ml
¼ cup = 2 fluid ounces = 50 ml	1 quart = 1 liter

252 Metric Information